ADVANCE PRAISE

"This book delivers an insightful examination of all things MBA. Capitalizing on relatable, real-life vignettes, it masterfully highlights key points for personal reflection to walk the reader through a holistic consideration process. Brian's voice permeates, creating an accessible text that flows like a [well-organized] chat with a friend who wants nothing but to support your success. A must read for everyone contemplating an MBA now or in the future—as well as those like me who strive to be helpful resources for these individuals!"

—Scott N. Paja, PhD, Director of Leadership and Professional Development, Oregon State University College of Engineering

"I have known Brian as an MBA student, fellow alumnus, and colleague for over a decade. Brian is a champion of the graduate student. His tireless work ethic, sincere and thoughtful strategies, and willingness to follow through have bettered the lives of hundreds, if not thousands, of students. When I had the opportunity to read his book, I was thrilled to find that he is now sharing those thoughts and strategies with prospective MBAs around the world."

—Mark Lockwood, Director, University of Illinois MBA

"Finding their career path is something I witness my students struggling with every day. Brian's book is invaluable to those considering an MBA; it is easily the most practical and useful guide to navigating business school and beyond that you will find anywhere. I only wish I could have read it before I began my MBA program!"

—Michael Fricke JD/MBA, Lecturer, College of Business, University of Illinois at Urbana-Champaign

"This is a very useful book for prospective MBA students, with solid advice given from someone who has spent years shepherding MBA students through their journey. While many books focus on getting in to an elite program, Brian Precious has written an excellent resource for maximizing your investment in any MBA program. It is well structured and an interesting read. A few hours reading this will really pay off in the long run for anyone considering (or in!) an MBA program."

—Christopher M. Barnes, Associate Professor, Michael G. Foster School of Business, University of Washington

"Getting an MBA is a major investment in terms of time and resources. An MBA degree from a good school not only prepares students for great jobs but also provides access to alumni networks that open doors for bright futures. While prospective students are aware that deciding on a specific MBA program is a significant (and highly personal) decision, they are often confused on the criteria to employ to make an informed choice.

By utilizing his personal experiences both as an MBA student and MBA program director, Brian Precious takes a prospective MBA student on an easy-to-read journey from the time getting an MBA is just an idea through desired post-MBA outcomes. The book is peppered with anecdotes and real-life stories that make it highly relevant to the reader. The result is a very thoughtful guide and a compelling read on how a prospect should select an MBA program that specifically works for them. This book is a must read for anyone considering an MBA."

—Rajagopal Echambadi, Senior Associate Dean-MBA Programs and Strategic Innovation, Professor of Business Administration, and James F. Towey Faculty Fellow at the University of Illinois at Urbana-Champaign

BRIAN PRECIOUS, MBA

GET IN, GET CONNECTED, GET HIRED

LESSONS FROM AN **MBA INSIDER**

RIVER GROVE
BOOKS

This publication is designed to provide accurate and authoritative information in regard to the subject matter covered. It is sold with the understanding that the publisher and author are not engaged in rendering legal, accounting, or other professional services. If legal advice or other expert assistance is required, the services of a competent professional should be sought.

Published by River Grove Books
Austin, TX
www.rivergrovebooks.com

Distributed by River Grove Books

Design and composition by Greenleaf Book Group
Cover design by Greenleaf Book Group

Cataloging-in-Publication data is available.

Print ISBN: 978-1-63299-083-9

eBook ISBN: 978-1-63299-084-6

Printed in the United States of America on acid-free paper

16 17 18 19 20 21   10 9 8 7 6 5 4 3 2 1

First Edition

To Sam
May you find your true passion
and use it to make the world a better place.
Love, Dad

CONTENTS

FOREWORD

The questions I most often hear from people who are considering whether to go to business school or not get to the heart of the matter quickly. They ask: Is it worth it? Is it a good idea for me? Can I get into the business schools I really want to attend? I've heard those questions for more than a quarter of a century, ever since I began writing about business schools as a journalist in the late 1980s at *Forbes* and *Businessweek* magazines.

Get In, Get Connected, Get Hired answers those questions better than any single book about business school or MBAs that I have ever read—and believe me, I have read a ton of them. This is largely because Brian Precious writes with great authority and clarity about the journey to and through an MBA experience and the likely outcomes that result from it. He has been in a great position to know. As an MBA admissions and program director, he has read thousands of applications, engaged in hundreds of admission interviews with jittery applicants, and crafted numerous marketing plans for schools to find and recruit the best students possible.

His astute observations come from an insider's knowledge of how an admissions committee evaluates the candidates who hope to get accepted into an MBA program. In the pages of this book, he strips away the mystery of the MBA admissions process, inviting us into a committee meeting to overhear the conversations that take place around the table.

If you're interested in getting an MBA but aren't quite sure the degree is right for you, read this book. If you've decided to apply, you will find Brian's candid and honest advice comforting throughout your personal journey to business school.

The truth is, getting into a highly selective MBA program is something of a marathon, from prepping for the GMAT or GRE to deciding which schools to target. Crafting an MBA application that effectively presents who you are and what you have achieved can be challenging for many. Landing a scholarship or grant to help ease the burden of the degree's cost can also be an art. Making sure your ultimate outcome—a more fulfilling and productive career that is right for you—is largely your responsibility.

Through each step of your journey, you would be hard-pressed to find a more empathetic and knowledgeable guide than Brian. He will help you determine whether the MBA is worth it. He will help you to understand if this degree is the right one to get you where you want to go. And he'll offer valuable insight on how to select the schools that will make it more likely to achieve your goals.

—*John Byrne*

INTRODUCTION

As soon as I answered the phone, I could hear the tension on the other end of the line.

"I don't get it. My grades and test scores are way above your averages. It's not fair."

I settled into my seat; this would be a long conversation. A recent MBA (master of business administration) applicant—I'll call him Andy—was calling to complain that we had denied him admission. As he ran through a litany of reasons that we were idiots who were making a huge mistake, I silently recalled the last time I had spoken to him. He had bragged shamelessly about all the exclusive programs that had accepted him. He had said we were his "safety school." And he had been completely unprofessional with our office manager.

"Tell me," he demanded. "Why didn't you admit me, anyway?"

I thought about the day the admissions committee met to review his application and how, despite his outstanding scores and grades, not a one of us wanted him in the program. I thought about telling him what one of my colleagues in career services had said at that meeting—that a personality like his would make it hard for her to place him at a neighborhood lemonade stand, let alone a top organization. Instead, I simply said, "I'm sorry. Our admissions committee felt you were not a good fit for our program."

With the right information, the right motivation, and the right approach, anyone can be successful in an MBA program.

A few days later, I got another call, this one from an admitted student. I remembered that her test scores and undergraduate grades had been unremarkable, but she had extensive work experience and outstanding letters of recommendation. Her interview was excellent. She had read up on the program and was excited about the school. I'll never forget the words of one of her former employers: "Shannon has the unique quality of making everyone around her better."

This time, it was excitement I heard over the phone line. Not only had Shannon been admitted, but she was also getting a generous scholarship. She was calling to accept her offer— and to thank us (and thank us, and thank us . . .).

In my career as an MBA admissions and program director, I've spent a lot of time thinking about Andy and Shannon. The difference in their (true) stories illustrates what I feel is a critical truth: With the right information, the right motivation, and the right approach, *anyone* can be successful in an MBA program.

I've come to this conclusion after building a career in MBA administration at three business schools, where I've read thousands of MBA applications, conducted hundreds of admissions interviews, created marketing plans to find and attract the best students, and advised students on how to successfully navigate the program. In the process, I've watched students leverage their MBA to change their careers and lives, and I've seen students waste time and money pursuing a degree that isn't a good fit for them. I've witnessed brilliant students miss out on job opportunities because they didn't know how to network, while students with average grades get offered six-figure career opportunities because of their great interpersonal skills and strong emotional intelligence. I've worked with students who have made their decision about which school to attend based solely on rankings, and I've met others who received generous scholarships to attend lower-ranked but still competitive schools.

By far, the best part of my job has been the opportunity to witness the way the degree can transform careers and lives. I've experienced this firsthand, having earned my own MBA at the University of Illinois. In a short 621 days, I had opportunities to travel the world, start a company, lead a major philanthropic effort, and serve as an elected student leader. I learned critical business concepts and equally important soft skills, built a valuable professional network, and made friendships that span the globe and have stood the test of time. My friends from the

Illinois MBA program have been my business partners, professional references, and international tour guides. I even met my wife through an MBA friend, and at our wedding, one of my classmates was a groomsman; another officiated the ceremony.

Along the way, I've met students from all walks of life, many of whom have incredible personal stories. But for each of them, I've consistently found that the difference between success and failure in obtaining an MBA—the difference between Andy and Shannon—boils down to a few common mistakes made at critical times in the process. These are—

- Lack of understanding about what the MBA is (and what it isn't)

- Lack of a clearly defined MBA strategy

- Overreliance on rankings in program selection

- Mismanagement of the recruiting process

- Misunderstanding of the admissions process

- Failure to negotiate on scholarships (or failure to negotiate well)

- Overemphasis on grades

- Engaging in acts of academic dishonesty

- Overreliance on career services in the job-search process

- Failure to stay connected with classmates and the school after graduation (a.k.a. failure to pay it forward)

In each chapter, we will explore these concepts in greater detail. I'll share specific examples of how these mistakes can derail even the hardest-working, best-intended students.

Drawing on my experiences both as an MBA student and as a program director, I'll offer some tips on better strategies and the questions you should consider in order to avoid these common pitfalls. Along the way, I'll share some insider perspectives on how you can stand out (in a good way) during the admissions and recruiting processes and, ultimately, as a student and alumnus of your chosen program.

Who Should Read This Book?

This book will be helpful if any of these situations apply to you:

- Someone told you to get an MBA, but you don't know if it's the right degree for you.

- You have thought about earning your MBA but don't know how to get started.

- You don't know how to find the best school for you.

- You have good grades and a great Graduate Management Admission Test (GMAT) score, but you didn't get in to your preferred business school and don't understand why.

- You don't understand how scholarships, grants, assistantships, and other means to fund an MBA education are allocated.

- You have just selected the school you want to attend and are looking for tips to maximize your student experience.

- You are getting ready to graduate from your MBA program and don't yet have a job.

- You mentor students and young professionals considering an MBA.

What This Book Is Not

Although we will certainly spend some time discussing best practices regarding the admissions process, this book is not intended to be an exhaustive resource on the following topics:

- Getting in to Ivy League schools

- Preparing for the GMAT or Graduate Record Examination (GRE)

- Crafting the "perfect" MBA admissions essay or personal statement

OK, we have a lot of work to do. Let's get started!

PART 1

GET IN

UNDERSTAND WHAT THE MBA IS (AND WHAT IT ISN'T)

It was my third meeting with "Joe" that semester. In our first conversation, I had broached the topic of his declining grades and suggested he hit the books a little harder. The second time, I had to tell him he was on academic probation and was heading down a path that could lead to his dismissal from the program. Today was going to be the toughest conversation of all. He was now failing three of his five classes, and several professors had noted his lack of effort coupled with a poor attitude in class. Just a few days ago, his classmates had requested that he be removed from his team because of his refusal to attend group meetings.

Although he certainly wasn't going to win any awards for maturity or emotional intelligence, Joe was a bright guy and had done very well in his undergraduate computer science program. His letters of recommendation discussed his passion for programming and praised his ability to learn new computer languages quickly and effectively. I wondered why someone who had learned to code in Java in less than a month would struggle so much in human resources, project management, and strategy classes.

I decided to skip my usual "You are in serious risk of failing out" lecture and instead asked him a series of questions. "Why do you think you are struggling so much lately?" (The classes are boring.) "Why don't you like your classes?" (They all focus on how to run a business or be a better manager. I don't want to be a manager.) "Do you think you are carrying your weight on your team projects?" (I don't like working in teams. I'm smarter than all of my teammates, and our group meetings just waste my time.) This went on for a while before I finally asked the right question: "Given your career goals, why did you decide to pursue an MBA?" He fell silent for a minute, considering my question, and then said, "My dad. He told me I should get my MBA so companies would pay me more." Bingo.

Unfortunately, this story does not have a happy ending. Joe dropped out of the program about six months before graduation and after shelling out close to $30,000 in tuition. He was out of work for about a year before taking an entry-level job he would have been qualified for with just his bachelor's degree. Not only did he lose time and money pursuing a degree that didn't align with his career goals, but by alienating his professors and classmates, he failed to enhance his professional network, which could have led to more-exciting career opportunities.

Joe didn't do his homework before starting his degree—a common mistake I've seen among prospective MBA students. You can avoid an ending like Joe's by taking some time to learn what the MBA degree really is (and what it's not) and to thoughtfully consider some alternatives to getting an MBA.

What Is an MBA?

MBA programs teach the business skills and provide the professional-development experiences necessary to help students become better managers and leaders. MBA students take courses in a wide variety of business disciplines, including accounting, marketing, operations, finance, statistics, human resources, and strategy. This coursework will help students learn some fundamental principles required to lead at a high-performing organization, but the real value of the MBA extends beyond the classroom. Integrated with the coursework are opportunities to engage in experiential, or applied, learning; to enhance professional development; and to develop a larger and more global professional network. A broad and versatile degree, the MBA is beneficial for people working in multiple sectors, including traditional for-profit businesses, nonprofit organizations, government entities, academic institutions, and new enterprises.

An MBA can help those without professional work experience land a meaningful first job. It can enable those looking to transition into a new industry or role to develop the skills, experiences, and contacts necessary for success. An MBA can also provide entrepreneurs with the tools they need to transform a promising concept into a successful entity. In some industries, an MBA will be either necessary or extremely helpful to those seeking senior-level positions.

Is an MBA Right for Me?

Each year I conduct exit interviews with graduating MBA students. One of the questions I like to ask is how the degree has benefited them personally. Following are some of my favorite answers:

- "I have a much better understanding of business fundamentals—what works and what doesn't and how to get there. I am much more confident in analyzing and solving problems."

- "I loved the hands-on learning opportunities. They helped keep my real-world skills fresh and earned me some great connections."

- "I used to be really nervous about managing other people. Now I feel like a confident leader who can manage teams of all sizes."

- "My knowledge of and appreciation for other cultures and styles of business will definitely serve me well at a multinational company."

- "I now have friends all over the world—I feel like I can find a job or a reference almost anywhere I go."

- "I've learned a wide range of communication skills and styles. I can confidently pitch a customer in an elevator or present to a CEO in a boardroom."

Clearly, these students maximized their MBA experience, starting with a thorough and thoughtful assessment of what the degree might bring to their careers. An MBA is not for everyone. It's difficult, time-consuming, and, in some cases, very expensive. On the other hand, for the right person, an MBA can be truly transformative. What's more, it can be a smart move at any stage in a career for people with or without a business background. An MBA might be right for you if—

- You desire a management or leadership role at work.

- You have a strong technical or STEM (science, technology, engineering, and mathematics) skill set and seek to transition from an individual contributor to a higher-level role within your current company.

- You want to start your own company.

- You want to change careers but lack the knowledge, connections, and experiences required for success in your new field.

- You want to advance beyond your current role but lack the skills required for promotion.

- You understand the importance of networking and value a global professional network.

- You are passionate about business, management, or leadership.

- You don't feel your undergraduate degree prepared you for the type of career you are seeking.

- You would like to work and live abroad at some point in your career.

What an MBA Isn't—Some Common Myths

If your reason for considering an MBA includes any of these common myths, it's important to separate fact from fiction before going any further. Pursuing an MBA as a result of these common—yet completely false—assumptions is a recipe for disaster.

"AN MBA IS A GUARANTEED TICKET TO A SIX-FIGURE JOB."

Although it's true that MBA graduates typically earn more than their non-MBA counterparts,[1] earning an MBA does not guarantee you a job, much less a high-paying job. The MBA degree provides a set of skills and opportunities that students must leverage to set their career on their preferred trajectory. Those seeking an MBA solely for financial reasons are often disappointed. Often, organizations willing to pay big bucks for top talent are looking for passion for the company, the industry, and the role.

"ALL I HAVE TO DO IS GET IN TO BUSINESS SCHOOL, AND THE PROGRAM WILL FIND ME A JOB."

Some students believe that once they get in to an MBA program, it's up to the placement office to find a job for them. While most placement offices have helpful staff dedicated to helping students maximize their career search, it is ultimately up to the students to create and execute their job-search strategy. Knowing the outcomes you desire before starting an MBA program can help you customize your experience—which classes you take, which activities you participate in, and which

---

1   Graduate Management Admission Council, "The Value of the MBA in 3D," 2014, http://newscenter.gmac.com/news-center/the-value-of-the-mba.

alumni you network with—thus increasing the chances of meeting or exceeding your postgraduation career expectations. We will cover this concept in more detail in Lesson 9.

"MY PARENT/PARTNER/FRIEND/BOSS/COLLEAGUE/HAIRDRESSER/ DOG WALKER SAID GETTING AN MBA HELPED THEM IN THEIR CAREER, SO EARNING AN MBA WILL HELP MY CAREER, TOO."

It's great to get advice from trusted friends and family, but it's also important that you personally see the degree adding value to your career and life. Earning an MBA takes time, effort, and money. For those who see the benefits, the sacrifices are well worth it. For those just going through the motions, however, working toward the degree can be an arduous process with mixed results. This is where Joe struggled. Joe's main interest was in computer programming, not leading a team or managing an organization. Although the degree may have helped Joe's dad advance his career, it was not the right choice for Joe.

"AN MBA IS ONLY FOR THOSE INTERESTED IN BUSINESS."

From running General Motors to starting a food pantry in your neighborhood, the critical success factors are more similar than you might think. You will need to understand your customers and how they wish to consume your products or services. You will need to motivate and manage your employees, you will need to comprehend how money flows through the organization and how new projects are funded, and you will need to know how to optimize your organization's day-to-day operations. An MBA can help in all of these areas.

Alternatives to the MBA

Before deciding if an MBA is right for you, you should explore some alternatives to earning this degree. Here are some ways to enhance your career without earning an MBA.

MORE WORK EXPERIENCE

Some feel the time spent earning an MBA can be better used by investing more into their current career. They believe taking on additional assignments at work will lead to faster promotions, a higher salary, and greater career-development opportunities. As long as the skills being gained are transferable to other industries, companies, and types of jobs, this strategy can be effective. Of course, staying at the same company also might limit your ability to enhance and broaden your professional network—one of the key benefits of the MBA.

CORPORATE LEADERSHIP-TRAINING PROGRAMS

Some organizations offer their most promising employees the opportunity to take leadership classes or to enroll in a management- or rotational-training program. These are great opportunities for those looking to stay at their current organization indefinitely, but such training doesn't offer the universal transferability and cross-industry networking opportunities of the MBA.

SPECIALTY MASTER'S PROGRAMS

Many business schools now offer specialty master's programs in fields that include accounting, human resources, business analytics, finance, and marketing. Compared to an MBA, these programs tend to be shorter and less expensive. They often have less stringent admissions requirements as well. Specialty master's programs can be good options for those who know they want to specialize in a certain field and aren't as interested in gaining proficiency in all aspects of business.

MASSIVELY OPEN ONLINE COURSES (MOOCS)

Through online education providers like Coursera and Udacity, students can now take free online courses in business and other disciplines. Some major universities are partnering with these online providers to offer a complete MBA degree at little or no cost. This is a great option for enhancing your technical skill set, but your experiential learning (learning by doing), networking, and leadership-development opportunities may not be as robust.

BOOT CAMPS

A newer option, boot camps offer short-term intensive coursework in traditional business disciplines, such as accounting, finance, or marketing. Courses typically run from ten to twelve weeks, and the cost is generally lower than that of an MBA. Boot camps are a great option for learning a specific skill. However, a single boot camp does not provide interdisciplinary learning opportunities and, compared with an MBA, will not be as effective in training you to become a better manager and leader.

Should I Work for a Few Years Before Earning My MBA?

One of the most common questions I receive from prospective MBA applicants is whether they should go straight from their undergraduate studies into an MBA program or work for a few years before returning to earn their degree. As with many questions in the MBA world, the answer to this one is "It depends."

Working for a few years before returning to school can be advantageous, especially if you plan to leverage your MBA to change careers. The combination of academic and experiential learning inherent to an MBA program can facilitate a career transition into a related or completely disparate field. Other advantages of waiting include the ability to bring real-world examples to classroom discussions and group projects, increased credibility with recruiters and employers, and greater flexibility in program choice, as some programs accept only those with work experience.

Entering an MBA program immediately upon graduation has some advantages as well. First off, being in "academic mode" eases the transition to graduate school (versus studying for the GMAT and taking a rigorous course load after being out of school for five or more years). Also, an MBA can positively differentiate you from your peers. Imagine how much more impressive you will be with an expanded knowledge of business fundamentals, opportunities to refine your leadership skills, and extensive experience working on group projects—often on multicultural teams. An early-career student may also focus more easily on the holistic MBA experience; older students, by contrast, often have to juggle work, family, and other commitments in conjunction with their studies.

The bottom line is that an MBA can be valuable, regardless of whether you decide to pursue it immediately upon graduation or after working for a few years. If you know an MBA is in the cards for you no matter what, it may be best to work for a while. However, if you are close to graduation and want to expand your career options, going right into a quality MBA program can be a smart career move as well.

Key Takeaways

In this lesson, we explored a common mistake—pursuing an MBA without really understanding the degree. We talked about the purpose of the MBA, some of its potential benefits, and common traits of those who effectively leverage its power. We also explored some common misconceptions, including the one that derailed Joe. Finally, we explored some worthwhile alternatives and discussed the pros and cons of working for a few years before earning the degree versus pursuing it immediately upon completion of your undergraduate studies.

Activity

Talk with at least three people in your professional network who have earned their MBA. Ask them why they pursued the degree, how they selected the school they attended, what they gained from the experience, and what advice they have to help you decide if an MBA is right for you.

Then talk with at least three people who considered an MBA but decided against it. Ask them to describe their thought process, what alternatives they considered, and the criteria by which they made their decision.

Reflection Questions

1. Do I understand the purpose of the MBA and what the degree can offer me?

2. Are my reasons for considering the degree consistent with its purpose?

3. Have any common misconceptions influenced my decision to consider (or not consider) the degree? If so, has my opinion changed? Why or why not?

4. Are any of the MBA alternatives listed in this lesson a good fit for my goals? Why or why not?

5. Considering everything I learned, do I believe an MBA is right for me? Why or why not?

6. If an MBA is right for me, should I apply soon or wait a few years? Why?

Now What?

Now that you have more knowledge about the MBA, you can use this information to avoid another common mistake. In the next lesson, we will talk about the importance of creating a thorough strategy for your MBA experience and examine how the failure to do so could impede your goals.

START WITH A GOOD STRATEGY

Unlike Joe, "Sara" was an excellent student and an even better team member. A human resources (HR) manager with more than ten years of work experience, Sara enrolled in our MBA for working professionals program to change gears and start a new career in marketing. Despite a busy full-time work schedule and numerous family commitments, Sara worked hard and earned almost all As in each of her classes. As graduation approached, I ran into Sara and offered my congratulations on her success in the program. I was shocked when she said, "Thanks, but I don't feel very successful. I decided to earn my MBA to start a new chapter of my career. Now I'm a month away from graduation, thousands of dollars in debt, and I'm no closer to a job in marketing than before I started."

"But Sara," I countered, with a mix of disbelief and concern, "students in our program with half your experience and work ethic have found great jobs in marketing. Have you talked with career services? Have you met with alumni in the field? Have you mentioned your goals to Professor 'Smith,' who used to work at Procter and Gamble? What about the marketing case competition[1] we hosted two months ago? The judges alone represented at least ten different potential employers."

She looked at me—I'm not sure if it was a look of annoyance or just plain exhaustion—and said, "I work fifty hours a week, have three kids, and for the last two and a half years have been going to class from 6:00 to 10:00 p.m. twice a week. When was I supposed to participate in a case competition?"

Despite her best intentions, Sara fell into a common trap. By failing to thoroughly think through her desired postgraduation outcomes, Sara made choices that obstructed her path to success. She chose an MBA format that left little time for working with career services and didn't provide the out-of-classroom experiences helpful for someone looking to change careers. She also didn't make time to network with other students, faculty, and alumni, and she chose not to participate in activities that would have allowed her to interact with potential employers.

Fortunately for Sara, these weren't irreversible mistakes. After graduation, she stayed connected with the program, joined the alumni association, and started

---

1   In a case competition, teams of business students compete to develop the best solution to a business problem. More on this in chapter 7.

coming to professional-networking events sponsored by our office. At one such event, she had a chance to reconnect with one of her professors. He introduced her to a former business partner, a step that started a chain of meetings ultimately leading to Sara's becoming a marketing manager at a local start-up company.

> ## Just as you wouldn't order bricks before figuring out how big you want your house to be, you shouldn't start applying to MBA programs until you think through exactly why you want the degree and what your desired postgraduation outcomes are.

Whether you are building a house, setting up a company, or considering business school, creating a comprehensive plan before getting started is critical. Just as you wouldn't order bricks before figuring out how big you want your house to be, you shouldn't start applying to MBA programs until you think through exactly why you want the degree and what your desired postgraduation outcomes are. Your answers to these questions will help you pick the right school and program for your specific needs.

Let's start with a basic question: What does finding the best MBA program mean to you? While this may seem like a simple question, there are actually many facets to a good match. For a program to be the best fit for your specific needs, consider the following:

- The program should offer an academically rigorous curriculum with specializations in the areas you want to work in after graduation. For example, if you want to be an investment banker, your ideal programs should be recognized for their finance faculty and curriculum. If you are interested in becoming a brand manager, your chosen programs should offer additional courses beyond the traditional Introduction to Marketing course.

- The program's format should be conducive to your lifestyle and post-MBA goals. Some formats maximize flexibility, while others allow for more interactive and outside-the-classroom experiences. Some formats are designed for those with professional work experience, and others welcome those coming straight from their undergraduate studies. We will delve further into formats in a bit.

- The program's extracurricular experiences should enable you to meet your stated goals. For example, if you want to work in management consulting and you don't have any previous experience in that industry, you may want a program that gives students the opportunity to work on consulting projects or to manage a student-run consultancy. If you want to work in another country after graduation, finding a program with a large international-student population and myriad study-abroad experiences is in your best interest.

- The program should offer the outside-the-classroom services you need to be successful. The best program for you will offer professional- and leadership-development opportunities best suited to your current level of experience and desired position after graduation. Your ideal program will offer career advice and alumni connections in the industries in which you are most interested in working.

- The program should be offered in the location that works best for you. This may be where you currently live or where you would like to live after graduation. In general, alumni tend to settle geographically close to where they went to school. Therefore, if you have a specific organization in mind as your future employer, it may make sense to consider programs geographically close to that company. This maximizes your chance of networking with hiring managers and decision makers within that organization while you are still in school. Of course, if you are pursuing online programs, location is not an important factor; but in most other situations, it should be a consideration.

- You should have a reasonable chance of being admitted to the program. Stanford University may have the best MBA program in the world, but if you are a C student with low GMAT scores and no work experience, it's not the best program for you. Although applying to a few "stretch" schools is usually a good strategy, it is also important to focus your time and energy on programs to which admission is a reasonable goal. (As we will see in subsequent lessons, you will need to invest both time and energy to fully research potential MBA programs.)

- You should be able to afford it. Earning an MBA is an investment, and you may have to take on some debt to complete your degree. You may be able to earn some scholarship funding or an assistantship based on the merit of your application; however, your expectations for scholarships should be in line with the programs you are considering. For example, a candidate with a 670 GMAT score, three years of work experience, and a 3.3 grade point average (GPA) could easily be denied by a Top Five school, admitted without a scholarship at a Top Twenty school, and given a substantial scholarship at a lower-ranked program. In general, students should expect to fund some of their MBA education. We will explore scholarships more in Lesson 6.

- The program should have the intangibles you are looking for. You should feel comfortable walking around campus. You should be proud to tell your friends and family you are considering that program. As you get to know the students and faculty, you should feel that you fit in and can thrive within the culture of the programs you are considering.

Sounds like a lot to ask for, right? It is, but with a little introspection and some legwork, I believe all prospective MBA students can and should find the best program for them. How do you get started? Here are a few tips.

Know Thyself

The more you understand your motivations for pursuing business school, the better the plan you can build. Start by thinking about your ideal post-MBA job. What industry are you working in? What type of organization are you working for? Is it a large, traditionally structured for-profit corporation or an innovative start-up? Do you want to start your own company?

Next, think about the type of role you would like. Are you interested in working as an HR manager, or would you prefer crunching numbers as a financial analyst? Maybe you want to work as a brand manager or a business analyst. What level of responsibility are you looking for? Are you more comfortable being an individual contributor, or would you prefer to lead others immediately? Do you want to be a functional expert or a generalist capable of leading multiple areas within an organization?

Now, what about location? Are you tied to a specific part of the country, or will you go wherever the best MBA program or post-MBA job opportunity is? Will you consider international opportunities? Are the industries and companies you identified earlier scattered throughout the world, or are there areas where several similar organizations are clustered (e.g., Silicon Valley for software companies and New York City for financial institutions)?

Now that you know what you want to do and where you may want to live, think about how the education, experience, and skills you already have align with your post-MBA goals. Are you considering an MBA to help you start your career, advance your career in your current industry, or help you transition into a new industry? Does your undergraduate academic background align with your goals? Do you have professional experience in the industries you are considering after graduation? Do you have any skills that may be relevant to the industries you are considering? This may include language skills, military experience, industry-specific training, or volunteer experience. Don't worry if the answer to most of these questions is no—that's why you are considering earning your MBA.

However, the more you will rely on your MBA to give you the experiences you need to transition into a new industry or role, the more important it is to choose a program and a format conducive to making this transformation. This is where Sara struggled.

The more you will rely on your MBA to give you the experiences you need to transition into a new industry or role, the more important it is to choose a program and a format conducive to making this transformation.

Next, think about how you plan to fund your education. If you are self-funding or relying on family support, you have the most flexibility on formats, programs, and locations. However, if your employer is funding some of your education, your options may be limited. How much are you willing to invest in your MBA education?

Finally, think about any constraints you may have. Will family obligations prevent you from going to school on the weekends? Do you have to complete your degree before a certain date? Are you planning to work full- or part-time while earning your degree? Do you have a limited number of hours per week to dedicate to your studies? Does your job require extensive travel?

Obviously, there are no right or wrong answers here, but thinking through these questions will help you determine the attributes that will make one program a better fit than another.

Pick the Right MBA Format for You

Thirty years ago, if you wanted to earn your MBA, your options were much more limited than they are today. Typically, MBA applicants in the '80s had an undergraduate degree in business or engineering and several years of work experience. There were a few hundred MBA programs to choose from, almost all of which required students to take two years off from work and enroll in a full-time program.

Today, the one-size-fits-all approach to MBA education has gone the way of acid-washed jeans, big hair, and the moonwalk. At last count, there were more than 15,000 business schools across the globe. New MBA programs attract students from different academic and professional backgrounds who are in various career stages and have diverse learning preferences.

More choices can lead to greater confusion. Many students with whom I work are overwhelmed by the number of MBA program options they have. The following is a quick rundown of the major MBA formats, their pros and cons, and my thoughts on which types of students are the best fit for each format.

❱ FULL-TIME MBA

Description: MBA program in which students attend class full-time during the day; typically involves students taking four to five classes per semester and takes eighteen to twenty-one months to complete

Also Known as: Two-year MBA, eighteen- to twenty-one-month MBA, on-campus MBA, early-career MBA

ADVANTAGES	DISADVANTAGES
• Students have more time to study and absorb class material.	• Students spend more time out of the workforce.
• Students have additional time for extracurricular activities (e.g., study abroad, club participation, case competitions) and job searching.	• Some coursework may be redundant for those with a business undergraduate degree.
• The format is most conducive to completing an internship between the first and second years of the program.	• Students must pay living expenses in addition to tuition.
• Students have the greatest opportunities for networking with classmates, faculty, and alumni.	
• Students can take full advantage of the career services/placement office.	
• This format offers the greatest scholarship opportunities.	

Best for: Younger professionals with less work experience who are seeking full-time employment in a new field or industry and looking for the most immersive MBA experience possible

❯❯ PART-TIME MBA

Description: MBA program in which students attend class during the evenings and/or on weekends

Also Known as: Evening MBA, weekend MBA, MBA for working professionals

ADVANTAGES	DISADVANTAGES
• Students can work full-time while earning their MBA.	• Some programs may be inflexible regarding family or work commitments during class time.
• Many companies offer tuition assistance to offset the cost of the degree.	• Part-time students may have difficulty interacting with full-time students and career-services/placement staff.
• These programs typically have the same professors and curriculum as the full-time program.	• This program takes longer to complete (typically two to three years) than a full-time or accelerated program.
• Students can immediately apply knowledge learned in the MBA program to their job.	
• Students have opportunities to network with classmates and faculty.	
• Many part-time programs offer GMAT waivers to exceptionally well-qualified applicants.	

Best for: Early- to mid-career professionals seeking a rigorous MBA experience while working full-time

❯ EXECUTIVE MBA

Description: MBA program designed for mid-senior career professionals seeking top management or executive leadership roles

Also Known as: MBA for executives

ADVANTAGES	DISADVANTAGES
• This format offers excellent professional-networking opportunities.	• This format is usually among the more expensive options.
• Typically, high levels of service (e.g., meals, lodging, and books) are provided to participants.	• Extensive work experience (five or more years) is typically required for admission.
• Some programs include perks like executive coaching or an international trip.	• Some programs may be inflexible to family or work commitments during class time.
• Many executive programs offer GMAT waivers to exceptionally well-qualified applicants.	

Best for: Experienced professionals looking for a high-touch MBA experience with ample opportunities for professional networking

❯❯ ONLINE MBA

Description: MBA program in which all learning and course-work is completed online. Initially, online MBA programs were largely offered by for-profit institutions, as opposed to accredited colleges and universities. More recently, established public and private universities have started offering their existing MBA programs in this new format. Choosing a program from a well-regarded university can offset some of the disadvantages of traditional online MBA programs listed below.

Also Known as: Distance MBA

ADVANTAGES	DISADVANTAGES
• Because the courses are online, students don't need to live near the university, they can study at a time and place most convenient to them, and no travel time or expense is required to get to class..	• Not all online MBA programs offer the same degree of academic rigor compared to competing full- and part-time programs.
• The online format can be less expensive than other MBA formats.	• Not all employers value online MBA degrees as much as full- or part-time programs.
• Entry requirements can be less stringent than other MBA formats.	• Students have minimal in-person interaction with faculty and classmates.
• Work experience typically is not required.	• Qualifications for teaching in some online programs can be less rigorous than for other formats.
• Some online programs do not require applicants to take the GMAT to be considered for admission.	

Best for: Professionals looking for the MBA option with the most flexibility; students who are very comfortable with self-paced learning and possess excellent time-management skills

❱❱ ONLINE-HYBRID MBA

Description: MBA program in which students complete the majority of coursework online while attending a few in-class sessions per course

Also Known as: Hybrid MBA, blended MBA

ADVANTAGES	DISADVANTAGES
• This format is flexible yet allows for face-to-face interactions with faculty and classmates.	• Students have to work or live close enough to attend mandatory in-person class sessions.

Best for: Professionals looking for the flexibility of an online program coupled with networking opportunities and face-to-face interactions with faculty and classmates

》 ACCELERATED MBA

Description: MBA program for students with an extensive business background—those who have taken business coursework or have hands-on experience; can be full- or part-time

Also Known as: One-year MBA, MBA for business professionals

ADVANTAGES	DISADVANTAGES
• This format takes less time and money to complete the degree than full- or part-time options.	• The compressed format may not work well for those without extensive business knowledge or with demanding work schedules.
• Coursework and projects tend to focus on more-advanced aspects of business.	• It has more difficult entry requirements than other formats do.
• Graduates typically receive the same degree as those in the full-time MBA program.	• Many programs require "prework" (e.g., completion of an online math course) prior to the start of coursework.
	• The format may not allow students to complete an internship.

Best for: Professionals with extensive business experience seeking a fast-paced, academically rigorous program

Implications

Now that you have had a chance to think about what you want to accomplish with your MBA and the different formats in which an MBA can be earned, let's look at how these factors influence the program selection of students in different situations. Following are real examples from prospective students I've worked with.

"ADAM"

Background: Adam just graduated with an engineering degree from a top school in the Midwest. He has no professional work experience, and his dream is to work as a marketing manager at Nike. He doesn't have any family or professional connections at Nike. He's planning on self-funding his education. He doesn't have any family obligations and is willing to relocate if needed.

Analysis: With no work experience, no connections, and a very specific goal of working at a highly selective organization, Adam needs a program with numerous opportunities for experiential learning and strong connections with Nike. Given he is self-funding his education, getting value for the money is also going to be important.

Recommendation: Adam should narrow his search to two-year, full-time MBA programs, preferably to those geographically close to Nike's headquarters near Portland, Oregon. Adam has no work experience, but choosing a two-year MBA will give him time not only to learn new skills in the classroom but also to participate in networking events and case competitions and to meet with as many alumni as possible. Given no constraints on where he goes to school, I recommend Adam pick a program close to his dream company. Thus, he'll have easier access to alumni from his chosen program who are currently at

Nike, and he'll also have time to build a professional network where he hopes to live after graduation. Adam also could pursue a highly selective, internationally ranked program with a top marketing MBA program. Schools like Northwestern (Kellogg), Pennsylvania (Wharton), and Stanford most certainly have the connections that open doors at Nike. However, they are likely to be among the most selective and expensive options for Adam and do not provide as much opportunity for him to build his network in Portland. In addition, many top-ranked programs do not admit applicants without work experience, and those that do almost never give them funding.

"BRANDI"

Background: Brandi has an undergraduate degree in business and has been working as a finance manager with a growing biotech start-up. She started with the company seven years ago and has impressed the leadership team with her knowledge of finance, work ethic, and willingness to take on new challenges as the organization expands. The CFO is getting ready to retire next year, and Brandi would like to be considered for the role, but she knows she needs to expand her skill set. The company is willing to subsidize the cost of her degree.

Analysis: Brandi needs a program that will facilitate her growth into a high-level role with her company. She's happily employed so will probably want to focus on non-full-time MBA options in her current location. She probably doesn't need to weight the quality of each program's career-services department as heavily as Adam should. However, she's looking to move into a C-level position, so finding a program where she can learn from more-experienced classmates would be a plus. Because her company is sponsoring her, cost doesn't have to be a top consideration.

Recommendation: Brandi should consider executive MBA programs in and around her current location. Executive MBA programs are designed for those either in or seeking top leadership positions within their organizations. While online or part-time programs could provide Brandi with helpful classes, an executive MBA program will provide Brandi with the best opportunities to expand and enhance her professional network with top business professionals. A downside of executive MBA programs is high cost, but this isn't as large of a consideration for Brandi, as her company is subsidizing her degree.

"CHARLIE"

Background: Charlie has an undergraduate degree in accounting and has been working as an auditor for three years. He's not passionate about his work and is considering a career in management consulting. He doesn't know much about consulting, but some of his best friends are in the industry and really enjoy the work. He's not sure if he should quit his job and go back to school full-time or if he should continue to work as an auditor while enrolling in a part-time evening MBA program.

Analysis: Given his business background and work experience in a competitive field, Charlie is likely to be an attractive candidate to many MBA programs. He's likely to earn a scholarship, so cost may be a secondary consideration. He would benefit most from a program that has strong connections in the consulting industry and provides opportunities to work in the field while he is a student. While a part-time MBA would allow him to keep working, career changers tend to benefit from formats that maximize experiential learning and networking opportunities.

Recommendation: With his business background, an accelerated full-time program may be best for Charlie. Such a program would provide time for networking and experiential learning but allow him to return to the workforce faster than a traditional two-year program. Several MBA programs own and operate consulting companies run by students, and Charlie may want to seek out programs offering this opportunity. Although he has friends in the industry, he may also want to pick a program with strong alumni and recruiter contacts in the consulting industry.

Career changers tend to benefit from formats that maximize experiential learning and networking opportunities.

"DANIELLE"

Background: Danielle is an entrepreneur who has been very successful with her software start-up. She recently spoke to investors about funding her company's expansion, but they said that they would prefer she have more business experience before they invest. She travels extensively and works irregular hours. Her main reason for pursuing the degree is to convince potential investors that she has the business acumen to run a successful company. She's invested most of her savings into her company and therefore doesn't have a lot to spend on her degree.

Analysis: Danielle needs a program that maximizes flexibility while minimizing cost.

Recommendation: An online MBA program would be the best fit for Danielle's schedule and budget. With an online program, she can work on her coursework at a time and place of her choosing. She can choose the pace at which she progresses through the program. Placement services, experiential learning opportunities, reputation, and alumni connections are secondary considerations. Danielle should look for a high-quality and affordable online MBA program with a specialization in entrepreneurship. She might also narrow her search to programs offered by accredited public or private universities as opposed to for-profit institutions, as this will give her degree the additional legitimacy desired by her investors.

Key Takeaways

In this lesson, we discussed the importance of creating a plan that outlines how earning your MBA will help you meet your specific career, life, and personal goals. We reviewed questions that can be used to formulate your plan and illustrated how your answers can help you determine which attributes should be most important to you as you start researching MBA programs. We also looked at the various formats in which an MBA can now be earned as well as the pros and cons associated with each. Finally, we looked at four different MBA applicants and determined that each one will require a vastly different MBA experience to meet his or her goals. No one MBA program, no matter how highly ranked, would be the best fit for all of the example applicants.

Activity

Utilizing the questions presented in this lesson, formally document your MBA "business plan." It doesn't have to be a novel; two to three pages is sufficient. Think through why you are pursuing the degree, what your desired postgraduation outcomes are, what format(s) work best for you, and how you plan to fund your education. This document will help you at every stage of the process, from identifying and researching programs through the recruiting and admissions processes and as a student in your chosen program.

Reflection Questions

1. What have I learned as a result of thinking through the questions outlined in this lesson?

2. Have I created a strategy consistent with my post-MBA goals?

3. How will this strategy affect the types of programs and formats I consider?

4. What format is best for me and why?

5. What programs should I consider and why?

Now What?

In the next lesson, we will explore some potential downfalls for applicants who rely solely on rankings—rather than their carefully formulated, highly personalized MBA plan—to pick a program.

UNDERSTAND THE RANKINGS AND USE THEM APPROPRIATELY

I try not to get too attached to students I'm recruiting, but "Juan" was someone I really wanted in our program. On paper, he was the perfect MBA applicant—great work experience and test scores coupled with strong academic performance and stellar letters of recommendation. He had done his homework and was considering our program because of our in-house consultancy, which is run by MBA students. He correctly assumed this would help him transition into the management-consulting field. In the interview, he was professional, confident, and did a great job establishing rapport. Like me, Juan was a car guy, and we spent a few minutes comparing notes on our favorite vehicles of all time. That afternoon, I convened our admissions committee, and we unanimously voted to admit Juan with a substantial scholarship.

A few weeks later Juan stopped by my office with some bad news. He wanted to let me know he had chosen another program. When I asked him how he had made his decision, he said, "I really love it here. Everyone is nice and the program aligns well with my career goals; however, I was admitted to a top-ranked program, and I don't feel I can turn down an opportunity like that." I asked if the program had any special resources for those hoping to work in consulting (no) and if the institution was offering financial aid (no).

Juan and I kept in touch. About two years later, he sent me an email to let me know he had just accepted an offer to work at a prestigious consulting firm in Chicago. Interestingly, it was the same firm at which we placed five of our graduates that year. I omitted this tidbit from my congratulatory note and instead asked if he was going to celebrate by treating himself to a new ride. He wrote back, saying, "Are you kidding? I have $120,000 in student loans. I'll be sticking with my Hyundai for a while."

It's probably unfair to call Juan's decision a mistake. He wound up with an excellent education and access to a diverse and powerful alumni network, and he was able to successfully transition into a better career. But could he have achieved the same outcome for a lot less money? Most likely. Like many prospective students, Juan used the rankings as the primary factor in deciding which MBA program to attend. Was this a good decision?

(If you end up in an MBA program, you'll quickly get used to this answer: It depends.)

The Good . . .

Rankings play a role in ensuring a basic level of quality standards across programs. With the growing diversity of the MBA degree, this standardization can be really helpful. Some have argued that lack of standardization allows less reputable programs to use false promises of easy or fast degrees to attract students. In an effort to outcompete their peer institutions, many schools use rankings as a benchmark for striving to increase the quality of their programming, often to the benefit of students. Furthermore, the rankings help encourage MBA-program leaders to stay on top of the latest trends in graduate business education, to the benefit of the entire industry.

The Bad . . .

Rankings tell only a small part of the story—just as most "objective" measures of an inherently subjective issue do. The MBA blog Poets and Quants[1] recently reviewed *U.S. News & World Report*'s peer assessments spanning a ten-year period and found little to no movement within the top twenty programs. This finding casts suspicion on the ranking system, especially when we consider that many institutions have added or eliminated programs and tracks, brought in new leadership, or completely changed their strategic direction in that time.

It is also important to remember that each ranking uses a different methodology and therefore yields different results. For example, in 2014 the University of Illinois (my alma mater) was ranked thirty-fifth by *U.S. News & World Report*, forty-fifth

---

1   Jeff Schmitt, "*U.S. News* Rankings: What Are Deans Really Assessing?" *Poets and Quants* (blog), July 21, 2015, http://poetsandquants.com/2015/07/21/u-s-news-rankings-what-are-deans-really-assessing/.

by *Forbes*, forty-fifth by *BusinessWeek*, and twenty-third by the *Financial Times*. It was unranked by *The Economist*.[2] So, is the University of Illinois a Top Twenty-Five powerhouse or an unranked—and therefore "unworthy"—program? It depends on where you look.

Rankings are also a lagging indicator. If you were to pick up a *U.S. News & World Report* ranking in 2015, the ranking would be based on data from the incoming class of 2012, which would have included students recruited during the 2011–12 academic year. That's a gap of more than three years between when some ranking data are collected and when that information is reflected in the most current version of the ranking.

And the Ugly

Schools may also take a number of statistical, shall we say, liberties in order to increase their quantitative scores. For example, if a school combines its full- and part-time placement data, the school's employment metrics would be artificially inflated, because part-time students are typically already employed. Or, because most rankings ask for the incoming class data as of the first day of the fall term, programs can require less qualified students to take a summer session, which keeps their academic profiles out of the reports sent to the rankings agencies. It is important to note that many of the major ranking agencies do not audit the data provided to them by MBA programs.

---

2 John Byrne, "Poets and Quants' 2014 Top 100 MBA Programs in the U.S.," *Poets and Quants* (blog), November 26, 2014, http://poetsandquants.com/2014/11/26/poetsquants-2014-best-business-school-ranking/4/.

How Should You Use the Rankings?

As I mentioned previously, I'm a car guy. According to my parents, the first magazine I ever read was *Car and Driver*, and it's still a favorite. I read several different auto publications on a regular basis and can usually quote each one's top picks. I enjoy reading expert reviews and learning as much as I can about the industry, but when it's time to make a purchase and my hard-earned money is at stake, I'm going to do a lot more than pick up a magazine to make sure I make the right decision. After learning my wife was pregnant, we decided it was time to trade in my ten-year-old sporty sedan for something with a little more room and a few more safety features. I read every article, review, and ranking I could get my hands on,

> At the end of the day, I made up my own ranking—one guided by consuming expert research but also by factoring in what is most important to my family.

but I also talked with everyone I knew who owned each of the vehicles I was considering. I then rented several of the models I had read about and consulted a mechanic to get his thoughts on the reliability of each model. Interestingly enough, after extensive research, I didn't buy the car that was listed as a best buy by *Consumer Reports*, and my selection wasn't highlighted as one of *Car and Driver's* ten best, but it was the car I felt most comfortable driving that met the needs of our growing family at a price I could afford. At the end of the day, I made up my own ranking—one guided by consuming expert research but also by factoring in what is most important to my family.

The same logic is appropriate for selecting the right MBA program. You'll want to include a review of the annual rank-

Be sure to spend plenty of time considering the factors that are most important to your goals, including format, location, culture, and, of course, cost.

ings in your research and use the rankings to ensure you're selecting a good program with a strong brand, but be sure to spend plenty of time considering the factors that are most important to your goals, including format, location, culture, and, of course, cost.

Here are some tips for most effectively using rankings as part of your decision-making process.

UNDERSTAND WHAT YOU'RE LOOKING AT

As you may already know, several well-known media outlets—including *U.S. News & World Report*, *Bloomberg BusinessWeek*, *The Economist*, *Forbes*, the *Financial Times,* and *The Wall Street Journal*—publish annual or biannual rankings highlighting the top MBA programs in the world. Each uses different methodology, but most combine qualitative survey data (from surveys completed by alumni, employers, and deans and program directors of other business schools) with quantitative data (e.g., average GMAT scores, average GPA, acceptance rate, and percentage of students employed at graduation) about each incoming and graduating class. These metrics—weighted differently depending on the ranking—are plugged into a spreadsheet, and voilà, we have MBA-program rankings.

For more context, let's take a look at the methodology for the 2016 *U.S. News & World Report* best business schools ranking.[3] I picked this one because it is most often consulted by domestic students considering earning their MBA. The following table shows what criteria *U.S. News & World Report* utilizes to determine top programs.

---

3   Sam Flanigan and Robert Morse, "Methodology: 2016 Best Business Schools Rankings," *U.S. News & World Report*, March 9, 2015, http://www.usnews.com/education/best-graduate-schools/articles/business-schools-methodology.

Methodology of U.S. News & World Report's Business School Ranking

INDICATOR	PERCENT OF TOTAL SCORE
QUALITY ASSESSMENT	**40**
Peer assessment (other business school deans or designates)	25
Recruiter assessment	15
PLACEMENT SUCCESS	**35**
Mean starting salary and bonus	14
Employment at graduation	7
Employment 90 days after graduation	14
STUDENT SELECTIVITY	**25**
Mean GMAT/GRE scores	16.25
Mean undergraduate GPA	7.5
Acceptance rate	1.25

CRITICALLY ANALYZE THE RANKING CRITERIA

OK, time for a quiz. Google the latest *U.S. News & World Report* top business school ranking, analyze the top picks, and think about the following questions:

a. Does the ranking favor private or public institutions? Why do you think that is?

b. Does the ranking favor urban or rural campuses? Why do you think that is?

c. How is a school's quality assessment determined, and how does the quality assessment help you find the best program for your needs?

d. Do the schools at the top of this list tend to place graduates in high-paying fields (e.g., finance or consulting)? Do you want to work in one of those fields?

e. Where is the school located, and where does it place the majority of its graduates? Is it fair to compare programs that place most of their graduates in large, expensive cities like New York and San Francisco with those that place many graduates in cities with a lower cost of living?

f. If you decide to attend a program that places many graduates into high-paying industries in expensive cities and this is not your goal, are you likely to earn the average salary upon graduation? If not, should you weight this metric heavily?

g. Are leadership, managerial, and interpersonal skills factored into the student-selectivity ranking? Should they be?

h. Should value for the money matter? Are costs represented in the rankings? Why or why not?

i. And now, for extra credit, review the *U.S. News & World Report* rankings for the past five to ten years. Has there been a lot of movement in top programs in that time? Why do you think that is? Are any new schools or programs listed in the Top Twenty-Five?

While there's no answer key for these questions, I have a few opinions on the topic.

DOES THE RANKING FAVOR PRIVATE OR PUBLIC INSTITUTIONS? WHY DO YOU THINK THAT IS?

Sixteen of the Top Twenty-Five programs[4] (sixty-four percent) listed in the 2016 *U.S. News & World Report* ranking of best business schools are private institutions. Do these institutions offer a dramatically better experience than their public school counterparts, or do biases in the methodology explain the disproportionate number of private schools in the Top Twenty-Five? While I have no doubt that Harvard, Stanford, Columbia, and the other top private schools offer wonderful MBA programs, I do believe a bias toward private schools exists in the *U.S. News & World Report* ranking. Public schools rely on state funding and, as a result, have a vastly different mission than their private counterparts. Well-funded private schools can focus mainly on selectivity, admitting only the most qualified applicants. Public schools, however, are incentivized to provide opportunity and access to education (particularly to underserved populations), to serve in-state residents, and to keep tuition as low as possible. This doesn't mean that public schools offer a lower quality experience; it just means they are at a disadvantage based on the selectivity criteria utilized by *U.S. News & World Report*.

DOES THE RANKING FAVOR URBAN OR RURAL CAMPUSES? WHY DO YOU THINK THAT IS?

Seventeen of the Top Twenty-Five programs (sixty-eight percent) are located in major metropolitan areas. Does this mean you will have a better MBA experience if you go to business school in a major city? I don't think so. It may mean that

---

4   Note that the *U.S. News & World Report* Top Twenty-Five for 2016 includes twenty-six programs as the result of a tie.

compared to rural and suburban campuses, schools located in a major metropolitan area are more likely to place their graduates in that city. Starting salaries tend to be higher in cities, but so do living costs. Urban programs may also, because of their location, have more visibility to the ranking agencies themselves.

HOW IS A SCHOOL'S QUALITY ASSESSMENT DETERMINED, AND HOW DOES THE QUALITY ASSESSMENT HELP YOU FIND THE BEST PROGRAM FOR YOUR NEEDS?

In my humble opinion, it doesn't. Each September, I receive a packet from *U.S. News & World Report* that contains a survey with the name of every MBA program in the United States that is accredited by the Association to Advance Collegiate Schools of Business (755 schools at the last count).[5] I'm asked to assign each program a ranking from 1 (marginal) to 5 (outstanding). Surveys from the deans and program directors who choose to participate (the overall response rate is about forty percent) are compiled into the peer-assessment score you see included in the ranking. As noted above, this very subjective process is worth twenty-five percent—more than any other single component—of the *U.S. News & World Report* ranking. So, the opinions of leaders at peer institutions (who may or may not have any current experience with the schools they are evaluating, or who choose to "punish" their direct competitors with unfairly low rankings) are the single most important factor in a school's ranking.

This is not to say that the top institutions don't deserve to be there, and it doesn't mean you shouldn't choose a Top

---

5   Association to Advance Collegiate Schools of Business, "Accredited Institutions," 2016, http://www.aacsb.edu/accreditation/accredited-members/.

Five program if it's the best fit for you. But there may be other programs—with lower peer assessments and therefore a lower overall ranking—that are a better match for your needs or your budget.

DO THE SCHOOLS AT THE TOP OF THIS LIST TEND TO PLACE GRADUATES IN HIGH-PAYING FIELDS (E.G., FINANCE OR CONSULTING)? DO YOU WANT TO WORK IN ONE OF THOSE FIELDS?

The employment report for Stanford University's class of 2014 is very impressive.[6] Almost every graduate was employed within ninety days of graduation, and the median starting salary was $125,000 (plus signing bonus and other guaranteed compensation). At least one graduate will be working in private equity with a guaranteed first-year income of $300,000. Pretty amazing for sure, but those numbers don't tell the whole story. Stanford graduates working in government have an average starting salary of $88,000 with one student accepting a job for $55,000 a year. If your goal is to work in private equity, going to Stanford may be worth it, but if your heart is in the public sector, even graduating from the number one MBA program in the world won't guarantee you a huge paycheck. Of course, salary isn't everything, but don't assume that you will receive a huge payoff upon graduation just because you attended a top-ranked program.

---

6   Stanford Graduate School of Business, *2013–2014 Employment Report*, October 15, 2014, https://www.gsb.stanford.edu/organizations/recruit/employment-reports.

WHERE IS THE SCHOOL LOCATED, AND WHERE DOES IT PLACE THE MAJORITY OF ITS GRADUATES? IS IT FAIR TO COMPARE PROGRAMS THAT PLACE MOST OF THEIR GRADUATES IN LARGE, EXPENSIVE CITIES LIKE NEW YORK AND SAN FRANCISCO WITH THOSE THAT PLACE MANY GRADUATES IN CITIES WITH A LOWER COST OF LIVING?

Perhaps it's a loaded question, but no, it's not fair to compare programs that place most of their graduates in expensive cities with those that tend to place graduates in smaller cities or suburban or rural areas. Why? Those who place many graduates in expensive cities will command a larger average starting salary than those who don't. This, as you will recall, helps their ranking in the *U.S. News & World Report* survey; however, those cities also have much higher living costs. For example, sixty-one percent of Stanford University's 2014 MBA graduates work in the western United States; the majority of them in and around San Francisco. However, if you choose to live in the City by the Bay, you will need that hefty paycheck to afford rent and other living expenses. According to *The Washington Post*, San Francisco is one of the top three most expensive U.S. cities in which to live.[7] Ranking solely on average starting salary without taking into account where the majority of graduates will be working not only skews the rankings but also paints a false picture of what your standard of living may be like after graduating. For example, while Stanford graduates earn a higher starting salary than graduates of Indiana University, if you took a job in Indianapolis for $100,000 per year, you would need to make $189,173 in San Francisco to

---

7 Jonnelle Marte, "The Most Expensive Cities in the U.S.," *The Washington Post*, August 26, 2015, http://www.washingtonpost.com/news/get-there/wp/2015/08/26/the-most-expensive-cities-in-the-u-s-for-single-people-and-families/.

have an equivalent standard of living.[8] The difference between the median starting salaries of graduates from the two schools is nowhere near that large ($125,000 and $104,000).

IF YOU DECIDE TO ATTEND A PROGRAM THAT PLACES MANY GRADUATES INTO HIGH-PAYING INDUSTRIES IN EXPENSIVE CITIES AND THIS IS NOT YOUR GOAL, ARE YOU LIKELY TO EARN THE AVERAGE SALARY UPON GRADUATION? IF NOT, SHOULD YOU WEIGHT THIS METRIC HEAVILY?

I don't want to beat a dead horse, but if you are looking at a program that is highly ranked because of a specialty in a field that is traditionally well paid (e.g., investment banking or management consulting) and you don't want to work in those fields, both the overall ranking and the average starting salary information is not going to be as useful for you as it would be for someone who is considering working in one of those fields.

ARE LEADERSHIP, MANAGERIAL, AND INTERPERSONAL SKILLS FACTORED INTO THE STUDENT-SELECTIVITY RANKING? SHOULD THEY BE?

Admitting students with a 4.0 GPA and an 800 GMAT score is very good for MBA programs, no doubt. The admission of such a student would positively affect almost twenty-five percent of the program's overall *U.S. News & World Report* ranking, but would it be good for you? It depends. If that straight-A student is also a great team player and brings to the program experiences that you can learn from, then sure. If not, being in class with a bunch of academically gifted students who lack professional experience or interpersonal and leadership skills is not in your best interest. As we discussed earlier, earning

---

8   Salary.com.

an MBA should be a truly immersive experience in which you learn not only from faculty while sitting in a classroom but also from your classmates and through practical experiences.

I'm not saying someone can't simultaneously be a good student, an exceptional test taker, a great team member, and a potential role model. However, the rankings—particularly those of *U.S. News & World Report*—incentivize programs to admit students who look great on paper, even if their interpersonal and leadership skills—which are harder to quantify—are lacking. In my experience, the greatest class discussions, group projects, and case competition teams happen when students from diverse academic, professional, and geographic backgrounds mesh as a high-performing team. Very rarely (honestly never) have I seen an exceptional team in which everyone was a top student and a GMAT whiz.

> **The rankings incentivize programs to admit students who look great on paper,** even if their interpersonal and leadership skills—which are harder to quantify—are lacking.

So, although the desire to go to an academically selective program is understandable, it's also important to have a feel for the student body. Reading the rankings alone won't provide that kind of insight. In the next lessons, I'll offer some tips for really getting to know the programs you are seriously considering.

SHOULD VALUE FOR THE MONEY MATTER? ARE COSTS
REPRESENTED IN THE RANKINGS? WHY OR WHY NOT?

If you pick up a copy of *Consumer Reports* or *Motor Trend,* you won't find comparison tests between a Ferrari and a minivan. The results of such a test would be meaningless. The two vehicles are in different price points, meet different needs (if you have four kids, a Ferrari isn't going to work for you, no matter how fast or gorgeous it is), and appeal to vastly different segments of the transportation market. So, what would be the point of ranking them? And if you did, on which criteria (trunk space or top speed) would you choose to base the rankings? The ranking criteria, not the respective quality of each vehicle, would dictate the winner.

Guess where I'm going with this. Pick up the *U.S. News & World Report* rankings and you will see programs with eight hundred students compared to programs with fifty. You see programs in rural Iowa compared to programs located in the heart of the financial district of New York City. You see programs that cost more than $100,000 compared to those costing less than $30,000. Yet they are all ranked on the same criteria, forty percent of which are extremely subjective and tend to favor expensive, private universities in urban settings.

AND NOW, FOR EXTRA CREDIT, REVIEW THE *U.S. NEWS &*
WORLD REPORT RANKINGS FOR THE LAST FIVE TO TEN YEARS.
HAS THERE BEEN A LOT OF MOVEMENT IN TOP PROGRAMS
IN THAT TIME? WHY DO YOU THINK THAT IS? ARE ANY NEW
SCHOOLS OR PROGRAMS LISTED IN THE TOP TWENTY-FIVE?

Think back to the year 1990 (if you are old enough). *Home Alone* was the number one movie in the country, and *Cheers* was our favorite TV show. If you wanted to get online, it was via AOL, and any music you bought (*Hold On* by Wilson

Phillips was the top song of the year)[9] was on cassettes or CDs. It would still be five years before you would send your first email and seventeen years before you could hold your first iPhone. Needless to say a lot has changed . . . except for MBA rankings.

In 1990, Stanford was the top-ranked program. Twenty-six years later the Cardinal still comes out on top. As a matter of fact, little has changed among the Top Ten.[10] While I have no doubt that all of the Top Ten programs were and still are wonderful, I find the lack of change in the rankings a little puzzling. Think of all the innovations that have occurred in the last twenty-five years—software, technology, medicine, transportation, space travel, and so forth. Think about how many new companies, products, and terms have entered our lexicon (people weren't *unfriending* each other in 1990) and how many are now gone (anyone still drive an Oldsmobile?). Why isn't the same level of innovation we've seen across virtually every other industry reflected in the *U.S. News & World Report* ranking of MBA programs? Why aren't there new players in the Top Ten? I think it has more to do with ranking criteria than actual lack of innovation. Many new programs have entered the industry, and it is now possible to earn an MBA through a much wider variety of formats. It seems likely that once a program has solidified a top position in the ranking, the heavy weight assigned to peer ranking ensures that that program stays on top. The question is, does this information help you find the best program for your needs? If not, how much weight should you give a program's ranking?

---

9   http://www.bobborst.com/popculture/top-100-songs-of-the-year/?year=1990

10   Matt Symonds, "A History of the *U.S. News* MBA Ranking 1990–2013," *MBA50*, March 25, 2013, http://www.mba50.com/a-history-of-the-us-news-mba-ranking -1990-2013/.

For an even more in-depth analysis of the *U.S. News and World Report* ranking, I recommend reading "The Order of Things"[11] by renowned author Malcolm Gladwell. His insights make an extremely compelling case for not placing too much stock on rankings in program selection.

DECIDE WHAT'S MOST IMPORTANT TO YOU

Now comes the fun part. It's now time to start thinking about the list of schools in your consideration set. Although this may seem like a daunting task, you have a framework to facilitate your efforts. By educating yourself on the real purpose and value of the MBA, you can feel confident you are pursuing the degree for the right reasons. Documenting your plan allowed you to think through the major decision criteria involved in school selection. Now you understand how programs are ranked and are in a better position to determine if and how they will influence the schools you decide to pursue.

There's no cookie-cutter formula here; if you are looking to work in a competitive industry at an elite firm and money is not a consideration, attending the highest ranked program you can get in to may be a smart strategy. However, a lower-ranked program with a unique specialization and the right alumni contacts may better meet your goals at a fraction of the cost.

Key Takeaways

In this chapter, we explored one of the most cited yet least understood components of the MBA program–selection process—the rankings. We learned that many rankings exist,

---

11   Malcolm Gladwell "The Order of Things", *The New Yorker*, February 14, 2011, http://www.newyorker.com/magazine/2011/02/14/the-order-of-things.

each with its own methodologies and data-collection processes as well as inherent biases and flaws. There is also great inconsistency among the rankings. As my colleagues like to say, "There are at least a hundred programs in the Top Twenty." (In other words, almost every program can point to at least one publication in which it is "ranked.")

Despite my strong opinions on some of their inherent flaws, I'm not against rankings. I believe they provide context from which to start the process of school selection. I am, however, against overreliance on rankings. Many prospective students choose the highest-ranked program to which they are admitted, but I've seen this strategy backfire as often as it has been successful. A far better strategy is to identify then aggressively yet intelligently pursue the schools with the unique combination of factors you need to be successful.

Activity

For each school you are currently considering, see how it is rated in each of the major MBA rankings (*U.S. News & World Report*, *BusinessWeek*, *The Economist*, *Forbes*, the *Financial Times,* and *The Wall Street Journal*).

Next, critically analyze the criteria utilized in each of the rankings, as we did with *U.S. News & World Report*. What patterns or inconsistencies do you notice? Which ranking criteria make the most sense to you? Why?

Reflection Questions

1. Do I now have a better understanding of the criteria utilized in the major MBA rankings?

2. What surprised me most as I learned more about ranking criteria?

3. How should/will I utilize the rankings in my MBA-program selection?

4. Which rankings will I weight more heavily in my analysis? Which ones will I weight less? Why?

5. Is attending a highly ranked MBA program important for achieving my goals? Why?

6. Based on the criteria I identified in Lesson 2 coupled with the data available in the latest rankings, which programs best meet my needs?

Now What?

Now that you know more about how to select the best programs for you, let's examine how you can get those schools excited about admitting you. In the next few lessons, I'll show you how to pursue your top schools in a way that helps you stand out from the crowd (in a good way).

USE THE RECRUITING PROCESS TO HELP YOUR APPLICATION

I almost have to give him credit. I'm pretty even-keeled, and it normally takes a while to get on my nerves. But "Robbie" managed to do so in under ten minutes. We were hosting a recruiting dinner for prospective students at a nice restaurant in Chicago. Robbie ambled in about forty-five minutes late, wearing shorts, sandals, and a Chicago Cubs T-shirt. I went up to introduce myself, and while shaking my hand, he asked if we had an open bar. Even though it looked like he'd already had a few, I pointed him in the right direction. When he returned, I asked about his background and if I could answer any questions for him. He told me that he'd come straight from the Cubs game and didn't have time to think of any questions. I learned he had been laid off and was between jobs. He thought an MBA would be a good way to change careers (he wasn't sure what he wanted to do next), but he didn't think he could afford it. He then asked about tuition and if he could have a scholarship. He concluded our already productive conversation by asking if I wanted to do a shot with him. I momentarily considered his request—if only to try to erase the last ten minutes from my memory—before politely declining.

It probably won't shock you to learn Robbie was not admitted to our program. Even if he had been an otherwise well-qualified candidate (he wasn't), it would have been difficult for him to overcome his first impression with the admissions team. Furthermore, by showing up unprepared and acting uninterested, Robbie missed out on a valuable opportunity to learn whether our program was a good fit for him.

While most of my interactions with prospective students are much more positive than my conversation with Robbie, there are some common mistakes students make during the recruitment process. In this chapter, we will explore them in more detail and offer better alternatives.

What Is the Recruiting Process?

I define the recruiting process as the *mutual exchange of information* between a prospective student and a program. Prospective students learn more about the programs by attending formal recruiting events; talking with students, faculty, and alumni; visiting campuses; attending classes; communicating with the admissions offices; and interacting with programs via social media. At the same time, admissions and program directors use the recruiting process to learn more about students they are considering for admission. We are using each interaction to gauge your interpersonal skills, judgment, and other intangibles that are sometimes difficult to ascertain from an application alone.

Goals of the Recruiting Process

As a prospective student, your goals during the recruiting process are very straightforward:

1. Learn as much about the program as possible so you can determine whether it is the best program for your unique needs and goals.

2. Make a positive impression with admissions staff, faculty, alumni, and others that may influence your admission decision and scholarship allocation should you decide to apply.

Learning about the Programs

With the help of the Internet, you can learn a lot about a program without ever leaving your couch. Most if not all MBA programs have detailed websites outlining the admissions process; curricular and extracurricular offerings; student, faculty, and alumni profiles; and job-placement statistics. In addition, each ranking agency has a website highlighting its top picks. These may be great places to start your research, but I encourage you to go beyond the web in your quest to learn which programs best fit your needs. Here are some other ways to dig deeper.

Engage on Social Media

Most programs have an active social media presence. Engaging with the programs on Twitter, Instagram, LinkedIn, and Facebook is a great way to learn more about the culture of the programs. Asking relevant questions, sharing your experiences, or (positively) commenting on stories, profiles, and blogs can help you connect with the key players. Noting the level of engagement from current students, faculty, employers, and alumni may be helpful in determining elements of a program's culture.

Asking relevant questions, sharing your experiences, or (positively) commenting on stories, profiles, and blogs can help you connect with key players.

One great example of this was a prospective student I worked with a few years ago. She posted a note on our LinkedIn alumni page, noting her interest in working at a specific company after graduation. Within a week, three alumni who worked at that organization reached out to her. One invited her to come to the office and personally facilitated an introduction to the HR manager. She wound up choosing our program in part because of how engaging and helpful our alumni were.

Attend Recruiting Events

Most schools schedule on-campus, off-campus, and virtual events throughout the academic year. These can be great opportunities to meet with current students and the admissions team. Be sure to connect with both the admissions staff as well as other prospective students during the event. Whether you decide to attend the program or not, recruiting events can be a great way to enhance your professional network.

Visit Campuses

While I know it's not always possible, I highly recommend visiting the schools you are most serious about. Why? It's the best way to explore the culture of the program. On a campus visit you can observe a class, talk with students and faculty, observe interactions among students and faculty, determine if you feel comfortable on campus, and see firsthand what a day in the life of a student is like. While on campus, be sure to meet with the career-services team to get a better understanding of the services they offer and the connections with companies and industries of interest that they can provide.

One of the most unusual requests I ever received was from an international student who wasn't able to visit our campus. Rather than relying solely on our brochure and website, he asked if I would give him a virtual tour of our facility. I appreciated his interest in our program and was more than happy to oblige. A few days later we connected on Skype, and I walked around the building with my iPad in hand. During his "tour," he sat in on a class, met three professors, and engaged with multiple students. The tour had a positive impact on him and was one of the main factors he used to choose our program.

Contact Current Students

Regardless of whether you are able to visit campus (or arrange for a virtual tour), you will want to speak with as many current students as possible. Many programs have student ambassadors who would be happy to speak with you. This is a great opportunity to ask more informal questions and can further your understanding of the organization's culture. You may also want to note the students' responsiveness, courtesy, and professionalism when you engage with them.

I can't recommend this strategy highly enough. Not only are current students excellent resources for information about the culture of a program, they also have knowledge of aspects of student life (e.g., where to live, the best restaurants on campus, and whether you will need or want a car) that you may find invaluable should you decide to attend. In addition, if you engage with current students, you will already have connections on campus if and when you attend that program. Even if you don't end up at that school, you've enhanced your professional network.

Contact Alumni

Through the admissions office, LinkedIn, or both, you should be able to get a list of alumni at companies or in industries of interest to you. I recommend reaching out with a professional note identifying yourself as a prospective MBA student and asking for a quick phone call or meeting. In my experience, many alumni welcome this kind of interaction and are happy to oblige.

Alumni are particularly helpful because they can share how their MBA has helped their career over time. They can also speak to the size, depth, and quality of the alumni network at that school. They may also be willing to facilitate introductions at their company or with relevant industry associations in which they participate.

What about Contacting Faculty?

Unless you have specific questions about a course they teach or a center they run, I don't recommend contacting faculty at this stage. Some students contact professors in hopes that faculty members will instruct the admissions office to admit them. That's not typically how it works. However, if during your campus visit you had a chance to attend a class, a well-written thank-you note to the professor is completely appropriate.

Now that we've talked about *what* to do, let's discuss *how* to do it.

Making a Good Impression

If you are going to take the time to really get to know a program, it's important to make a positive impression during all of your interactions. Here are some tips to ensure this time spent helps your chances of admission.

Do

- Be positive with everyone you meet, including student workers, other prospective students, administrative staff, and those in other areas of the university (e.g., housing and financial aid). Assume they all either directly or indirectly can influence your admission decision. In many cases, they do. I remember a situation in which our admissions committee was lukewarm on an applicant and was strongly considering wait-listing her. While reviewing her file, I came across an email correspondence between the applicant and one of our student workers. I asked the student worker about this applicant, and he said she was extremely professional and seemed very interested in our program. He mentioned that she sent him a card to thank him for all of his help with the admissions process. This new information was enough to tip the scales in favor of admitting her. Treating our student worker professionally and respectfully made all the difference for that applicant.

- Show up on time and dress appropriately for the situation. When in doubt, err on the side of being overdressed as opposed to the sandals-and-Cubs-shirt look. When a prospective student shows up dressed unprofessionally to a recruiting event or campus visit, it causes concern. Why do we care? Eventually, this same student, if admitted, is going to be introduced to alumni, recruiters, and other friends of the college. How that student dresses and acts reflects on the program.

- Keep all emails and social media posts positive and helpful. A great example of this was a student who posted a picture of her posing with our school's mascot to our Facebook page. Along with the picture was a quick note about how much she enjoyed her campus visit. To me, this demonstrated a sincere interest in our program, and this enthusiasm was noted by the admissions committee.

- Learn as much as you can about the program before interacting with the stakeholders. Taking time to learn the names of buildings, program-specific acronyms, specializations, and other aspects of campus life implies genuine interest.

- Send personalized thank-you notes to anyone who facilitated your information-gathering process. It's a small touch, and most don't take the time to do it; however, if it is done well, it can positively differentiate you.

Don't

- Don't focus on scholarships at this stage. You don't want to give the impression that you are interested only if you get a scholarship. Instead, use your time with the program to explore fit. There will be plenty of time to discuss financial arrangements after you are admitted. Hopefully, by following some of the advice in this lesson, you have put yourself in the best possible position for a successful negotiation later.

- Don't spend a lot of time asking basic questions that can be answered by visiting the program's website. Doing so signals either a lack of interest, lack of preparation, or both.

- Don't bring gifts to recruiting events or campus visits. Some prospective students do this with the most benevolent of intentions, but it creates an awkward situation for the admissions team.

- Don't contact the admissions office excessively. Generally speaking, hearing from prospective students before they apply demonstrates interest, which is a good thing. However, too much of a good thing can backfire. Be respectful of the admissions team's time, especially during the busiest parts of the recruiting cycle.

Key Takeaways

Both prospective students and programs benefit from the recruitment process. Students have the opportunity to go beyond a program's website and explore the people and culture in more detail. Programs utilize recruitment activities to see which prospects have intangible qualities that make a good student, team member, alumnus, and employee—attributes that are sometimes more difficult to determine from the application alone.

The more time and effort you dedicate to learning about the programs in your consideration set, the better. This investment ensures that you pick a program that not only looks great in the rankings or has a shiny website but also is best suited to your career goals, needs, and personality. Several ideas for going beyond Internet research are outlined in this lesson.

It's also important to use the recruiting process as an opportunity to positively differentiate yourself. Those demonstrating professionalism, emotional intelligence, and genuine interest in a given program create advocates on the admissions committee. Conversely, those who don't—like my friend Robbie—create self-inflicted barriers to admission.

Activity

Plan a campus visit to the school you are most excited about. Think through what you hope to accomplish and how you plan to make this happen. What questions do you have? What do you hope to learn about the culture of the program? Are there any specific centers, activities, or classes you would like to experience? If possible, reach out to current students beforehand and ask to meet with them informally during your visit.

Make sure your visit includes a trip to the placement office, the alumni center, and a student-club meeting or event.

Research the program thoroughly before your visit, and develop some questions for each of the stakeholders you are likely to meet. After your visit be sure to send thank-you notes and to follow up on anything you said you would do.

Reflection Questions

1. What information not available online would I like to know about my top schools?

2. How can I ascertain this information?

3. What information should I know about the programs I'm interested in before visiting campus or attending a recruiting event?

4. If an in-person campus visit is not possible, how will I learn about the program I am considering?

5. How can I positively differentiate myself during the recruiting process?

Now What?

In the next lesson, we'll explore the application process, identifying common mistakes and alternative strategies that move you closer to being admitted to your dream school.

UNDERSTAND AND OPTIMIZE THE ADMISSIONS PROCESS

Poor "Jane." She was probably the most determined applicant I wasn't able to admit. Jane was an international student with nearly perfect grades from a well-known university. Her father had attended our school, and it was her dream to follow in his footsteps. Jane decided to wait until the end of the admissions cycle to give herself time to take the GMAT for a sixth time. While her score was in the right ballpark, the rest of her application fell short. Her essays were generic and suspiciously resembled those from other applicants. Her letters of recommendation offered no detail and could have been written about any applicant.

As is often the case with an applicant who has strong grades and test scores but an otherwise-weak application, it all came down to the interview. Jane was very polite and was able to convey her strong desire to attend our program, but when asked for examples demonstrating her leadership abilities, she stumbled. When questioned about her thoughts on teamwork, she said she preferred to work alone. When asked to demonstrate her impact either at work, school, or with a volunteer organization, she couldn't answer the question. She ended the interview by assuring me she would get all As in her classes if she was admitted.

A few days later, the admissions committee met for the final time that year. We were down to seven viable candidates competing for the three remaining spots in the class. There were some strong arguments for admitting her—a female candidate with great grades and test scores would surely help our class profile. Yet ultimately, after a thoughtful debate, we offered the remaining spots to other candidates.

Although it was the right call, not admitting Jane still bothers me. Had she better understood the admissions process and made just a few changes in her strategy, she probably would have had the opportunity to attend her dream school. To learn from Jane's mistakes, let's take a detailed look at the admissions process, from both the applicant and program perspectives.

What Is the Admissions Process?

Many applicants think the application process comprises the tactical completion of a series of tasks required for admission to business school. They believe once those tasks are completed, applying to multiple schools is a simple cut-and-paste process. Other applicants suspect that of the numerous admissions requirements, only the quantitative elements—GMAT score and GPA—really matter. Neither hits the mark; the process is much more complex and nuanced.

> The admissions process is about showcasing the intangibles—ethics, interpersonal skills, selflessness, leadership potential, and emotional intelligence—required to lead in today's complicated, global business ecosystem. The process should be an authentic glimpse at who you are and who you want to be.

The admissions process is really about storytelling. It's about illustrating how your goals align with the strengths of your desired program. It's about weaving together seemingly disparate components—test scores, letters of recommendation, and essays—into a compelling narrative highlighting not only your ability to succeed academically but also your desire to be a lifetime contributor to the institution's community. It's about showcasing the intangibles—ethics, interpersonal skills, selflessness, leadership potential, and emotional intelligence—required to lead in today's complicated, global business ecosystem. The process should be an authentic glimpse at who you are and who you want to be. Most importantly, the admissions process is an *opportunity to differentiate yourself* from the hundreds, if not thousands, of other applicants that may have similar grades and test scores.

What I Look For When I Review Applications and Conduct Interviews

The application process is arduous for applicants and programs alike. Prospective students spend months preparing for and taking the GMAT, writing essays, talking with their recommenders, and practicing for their interviews. On the other side of the admissions office, it takes several hours to properly review each application, prepare for and conduct an interview, compile notes, and be ready to discuss the applicant in detail during the admissions committee review. The process is probably more complicated than it needs to be.

For me, the whole process boils down to a few basic questions. The better I feel about the answers to these questions, the more likely I am to recommend admission. After reviewing the application and conducting an interview, if I still don't know the answers to these questions, or don't like the answers, it becomes much harder for me to recommend the student for admission to our program. Note, I said "much harder," not "impossible." We sometimes admit students we aren't completely comfortable with for various reasons. However, by better understanding the process, you put yourself in a position to develop a high-quality application, which increases your odds of not only admission but also financial aid (more on this in the next lesson).

Granted, every school is different, and even different admissions officers within the same program may have slightly different approaches. Still, I believe all applicants can positively differentiate themselves and optimize their chances for admission by understanding this framework when developing their application.

QUESTION I: WILL THE APPLICANT BE SUCCESSFUL ACADEMICALLY?

The last thing I want to do is set students up for failure by admitting them to a program when they don't have the academic skills necessary for success. It's very important that students are successful because successful students become engaged alumni. Engaged alumni help our program get better over time by mentoring students, providing job and internship opportunities, and sharing their professional skills with our students.

To gauge whether a student will be able to handle the rigor of our program, I typically review transcripts, test scores, and letters of recommendation. The perfect applicant would have a strong GPA from a well-known and academically rigorous university in a scientific, engineering, math-related, or business field. These credentials—coupled with a strong GMAT score and a letter of recommendation from a respected faculty member confirming the student's work ethic and ability to master new tasks quickly—would make for a very strong application. Bonus points may go to an applicant with a master's or PhD in a related field or to someone with extensive work experience in a field requiring the constant learning of difficult concepts (this would be ascertained from the resume and the letters of recommendation).

Of course, no applicant is perfect. If you have lower grades, or decent grades in a nontechnical field, I'm going to look more heavily at your GMAT score—particularly the quantitative section—than I would if you had a 3.8 GPA in computer engineering from the Massachusetts Institute of Technology. If your overall GPA is low but your grades improved over time, that's better than the other way around. In that case, it demonstrates a more recent pattern of academic success. If your undergraduate grades are low but you have been successful taking courses more recently, that can help assure me you will be academically successful. Also, the longer you have been out of school, the more your professional experience and letters of recommendation outweigh your grades. However, if you are hoping to join our program straight out of your undergraduate studies, your grades are going to be weighted heavily, since I don't have a lot of other information (e.g., work experience) to guide my decision.

QUESTION 2: ARE THE APPLICANT'S POST-MBA GOALS CLEARLY DEFINED? DO THEY ALIGN WITH THE STRENGTHS OF OUR PROGRAM?

Again, my goal is to admit students who are going to be successful both in the program and beyond. Those who come in focused and interested in an area that aligns with our school's strengths are likely to have a great experience, making the program better for their classmates and leaving with an excellent job offer (or several). Those lacking focus are more likely to struggle academically and not connect with classmates, alumni, and potential employers.

To determine fit and alignment with our program, I look carefully at essays and letters of recommendation and ask several detailed questions during the admissions interview. In the essays and personal statement, I'm looking for a well-written and clearly articulated description of your post-MBA goals, along with a detailed description of why our program is well suited for helping you achieve those goals. The more you mention specific faculty, alumni, or programmatic offerings unique to us, the better. Accidently using the name of another school is a huge red flag.

In the letters of recommendation, I'm looking for confirmation of your goals and examples of how these goals align with your strengths and previous experiences. For example, if your goal is to find a job in management consulting, it is very helpful if at least one of your recommenders offers detailed examples of your problem-solving and customer-service skills, as well as your ability to think on your feet. Reinforcing these themes during the interview helps solidify that you are certain of what you want to accomplish and can articulate the reasons our program is best able to help you meet your goals.

I get concerned if you either don't know why you want to earn your MBA or are considering an MBA for the wrong reasons (e.g., you want to be guaranteed a job). It's also disconcerting if your goals don't match the strengths of our program. I once worked with a prospective student who wanted to work in investment banking. We didn't offer any special courses in investment banking and neither our career-services team nor our alumni association had any connections with major investment banks. Although he was otherwise qualified for admission, I encouraged him to research other schools that had resources more closely aligned with his end goal. Remember, we strive for one hundred percent placement and one hundred percent student satisfaction with the MBA experience. These goals not only help with our rankings but also result in word-of-mouth from happy students and alumni, which is a big part of any successful program's recruiting strategy. If I don't honestly believe we can help students achieve their goals, it's very hard for me to recommend admitting them, regardless of their qualifications.

QUESTION 3: CAN THE APPLICANT COMMUNICATE EFFECTIVELY, BOTH ORALLY AND IN WRITING?

Communication skills are of critical importance, both during the program and beyond. Being able to cogently articulate an argument, clearly document findings and recommendations, and develop a high-impact presentation are requirements for success in any MBA program. More important, these skills are required by employers everywhere. According to a recent study conducted by *Bloomberg Businessweek,*[1] excellent communication skills are among the least common but most desired skills across all industries.

To gauge communication skills, I review the essays and personal statement, of course. But I also consider all communications the applicant has had with our team. Sending a terse or unclear email to a student worker or administrative professional is a red flag for me. So are essays or personal statements that contain multiple spelling and grammar mistakes. The biggest red flag of all is an essay that does not appear to have been written by the applicant.

Conversely, applicants who write articulately and communicate with everyone in a professional manner do themselves a lot of good in the admissions process. It's also helpful if the letters of recommendation specifically mention communication skills as a strength. Bonus points go to the applicants who follow up by sending a personalized thank-you note after an admissions event or interview.

---

1   Francesca Levy and Jonathan Rodkin, "The Bloomberg Recruiter Report: Job Skills Companies Want But Can't Get," *Bloomberg*, 2015, http://www.bloomberg.com/graphics/2015-job-skills-report/.

QUESTION 4: DOES THE APPLICANT DEMONSTRATE LEADERSHIP POTENTIAL?

This is probably one of the most important questions I ask when reviewing an application. As we've already discussed, MBA programs are designed to help those who wish to lead organizations. Good leaders are so important yet so rare. My goal is to identify and prioritize the admission of those who can demonstrate they are already good leaders or those who can show they have the desire and potential to become good leaders.

So, where do I look for evidence of leadership skills or potential? The personal statement and essays are important. In these, I'm looking for evidence that you have made a positive impact on the organizations and companies with which you've been affiliated. I'm not expecting a twenty-four-year-old to have run a major corporation, but I would like to see that you have been active in student organizations. If you have served in meaningful leadership positions in those organizations, you are in good shape. In the essays, I'm also looking for information about your leadership style. Writing about your thought process as you faced a tough problem or how you brought people with differing beliefs together can be a positive differentiator. I'm also looking for examples of how you intend to enhance the student learning community. Mentioning your desire to participate in or lead specific clubs, or talking about starting a new one, demonstrates your intent to lead as a student.

Letters of recommendation are also important. If your letters of recommendation offer vivid examples of your ability to serve others above yourself, you are well on your way to demonstrating this critical skill. Of course, if you have already had the opportunity to lead others in a professional setting, describing these experiences in detail and asking your recommenders to comment on the results of your actions can be extremely beneficial to you.

Some applicants make the mistake of talking about all of their accomplishments without giving credit to others. I once interviewed an applicant who told me his company tasked him with launching a new product in his native country. From his description, you would have thought he developed the product himself, set up the distribution network, created the advertising campaign, and personally delivered the product to new customers. When I dug deeper, I learned he was part of a thirty-person exploratory team tasked with identifying the benefits and risks of bringing a new product to this country. His actual role was to compile the research and document the findings and recommendations. Obviously, this was a red flag, since true leaders help others achieve their full potential without worrying about who gets the credit.

It's also a bit of a concern if an applicant has no extracurricular or volunteer experience either as a student or young professional. While I value those with excellent academic credentials or significant professional accomplishments, I also appreciate those who have volunteered their time and talents to benefit others. Of course, the quality of the engagement is more important than the number of charities, clubs, or civic organizations with which an applicant is involved. I would much rather see an applicant take a leadership role and be able to demonstrate a positive and meaningful impact with one or two organizations than attempt to "check the box" by listing several organizations in which the participation is less involved and effective. I once interviewed an applicant who had listed involvement with about ten charitable organizations on her resume. When I asked her about one with which I wasn't familiar, she told me she couldn't remember what she had done for that charity. Not good!

QUESTION 5: DOES THE APPLICANT'S CONDUCT INDICATE ETHICS AND A SENSE OF HONOR?

Sadly, it's not hard to think of numerous examples of unethical leaders destroying companies, defrauding investors, and harming their customers. MBA programs tend to place graduates in leadership positions, and I see it as a moral obligation to verify that those I am considering for admission to our program have a solid understanding of the importance of ethical behavior.

To answer the question of whether I believe the applicant will behave ethically, I utilize every aspect of the application. I look at the essays and letters of recommendation to see if the applicant has ever been placed in a difficult ethical situation and learn what the response was. I also carefully review the essays to verify that they were actually written by the applicant. On occasion, I've phoned a recommender to get additional details about some information depicted in a letter of recommendation. Every now and then, I've come across a made-up letter of recommendation (either the supposed recommender or company doesn't exist) and this always, always, always leads to an immediate denial of admission, regardless of the applicant's other qualifications.

The best advice I can give is to demonstrate your understanding of the importance of ethics in business school and beyond. Talk about difficult situations you have faced, and walk the reader through your thought process, the actions you took, and the results.

QUESTION 6: WILL THE APPLICANT BE A GOOD TEAM MEMBER? WOULD I WANT TO BE ON A TEAM WITH HIM OR HER?

Like communication skills, the ability to be an effective team member is a critical success factor both in business school and in the "real world." I would much rather have someone in my program who has lower grades or test scores but has exceptional interpersonal skills and an orientation toward teamwork than the other way around.

It's pretty easy to spot good team players. They tend to use *we* more than *I* in their essays and during their interviews. Their recommenders highlight their team-oriented nature and offer examples illustrating their ability to function in a highly collaborative environment. Some applicants bring to the interview a portfolio of group projects on which they have worked.

It's equally easy to spot those who aren't team players. They tend to talk about themselves constantly and struggle when asked questions about their role in group projects. They often take credit for the successes of the team and blame failures on others. They also tend to interrupt constantly and exhibit other rude behavior while interacting with our team at recruiting events and during the admissions interview.

As an MBA student, I once had a crazy week in which three group projects, two presentations, and a case competition all were due within a few days of each other. Our team spent more than sixty hours together in a breakout meeting room with very bad coffee and a lot of fast food. It was an extremely stressful time, but somehow we completed all of our assignments on time with a high degree of quality. All the team members pulled together and utilized their individual strengths to the benefit of the team as a whole. I remember feeling extremely fortunate to have such professional and capable teammates. When I'm conducting admissions interviews, I often think back to that week and ask myself if I would have wanted the person I'm interviewing on our team with us. The answer to that question sometimes carries more weight than the applicant's GMAT score, grades, or undergraduate GPA.

QUESTION 7: WILL THE APPLICANT BE EMPLOYABLE AT THE END OF THE PROGRAM? WOULD I HIRE HIM OR HER?

Applicants may have excellent grades, test scores, and other credentials, but if they aren't likely to be employable by graduation, it's hard to get excited about admitting them. What does *employable* mean? It means having the technical skills—such as an understanding of marketing, accounting, or finance—coupled with the intangibles needed for success in today's interconnected and increasingly complex global workforce. These intangible qualities include interpersonal, leadership, and communication skills; work ethic; maturity; ability to work on multicultural teams; and a strong ethical compass.

Why is employability important? Well, as you learned in Lesson 3, it helps our rankings, but that's not the most important reason. Those who leave their MBA program with at least one job offer are more likely to be satisfied with their overall experience. Satisfied graduates tend to stay engaged and help enhance the program as alumni. An engaged alumni base makes my job much easier. Alumni help me recruit prospective students, mentor current students, and identify job and internship opportunities at their organizations.

I look at all components of the application to gauge employability. The quantitative elements (e.g., grades and test scores) help me understand the applicant's ability to be successful in a competitive environment, while the essays and personal statement highlight communication skills, thought processes, and the ability to make a persuasive argument.

Letters of recommendation, particularly from previous or current employers, help me better understand the applicant's personality, work ethic, and ability to thrive in a professional environment. In the interview, I try to determine drive and motivation and consider whether I believe the applicant will be impressive to future employers. Just as I ask myself whether I would have wanted the applicant on my team during our "hell week," I also often ask if I would want to work daily with the person I'm interviewing.

QUESTION 8: DOES THE APPLICANT SPECIFICALLY WANT TO ATTEND OUR PROGRAM? WILL INVOLVEMENT IN THE PROGRAM CONTINUE BEYOND GRADUATION?

I would much rather admit a student with lesser quantitative qualifications but a great desire to attend our program than the other way around. I can usually tell from the essays and definitely from the interview whether applicants are passionate about my school or if they see it as just another MBA program they will attend if the price is right.

Why do I care if a student is passionate about our program? Passion is infectious. In my experience, those who are excited about attending our program usually earn better grades, work harder, get more involved with extracurricular activities, and have a better experience than students who pick their program based on rankings, cost, or which one gave them the largest scholarship. They are also much more likely to stay involved as alumni and give back to the program.

It's pretty obvious when an applicant is excited about our program. After a while it gets pretty easy to tell the difference between an applicant who has tailored their application specifically for our program and one who has cut and pasted the name of our school into the appropriate places in the essays and personal statement. The distinction becomes even clearer when the applicant submits essays with the wrong school name. As you can probably imagine, this is a huge turnoff. While I have sometimes had to admit people who have made it clear that we weren't their first choice, these folks usually don't get our best scholarship offer. We try to save our top awards for those who are qualified and sincerely want to be a part of our community.

BACK TO JANE

So, using this framework as a guide, let's take a closer look at how well Jane did in the admissions process.

1. Did Jane demonstrate that she could handle the academic rigor of our program? Absolutely. She had excellent grades from a great university in a technical field. In addition, she had a very strong GMAT score, particularly in the quantitative section. I have absolutely no doubt that she will be successful in her classes.

2. Are Jane's career goals well outlined, and do they correspond with the strengths of our program? Because her essays and letters of recommendation were generic, I'm not sure. She talked about wanting to work in the United States for a few years before returning home to join the family business. She didn't say what she wanted to do and didn't tie it back to our program. I definitely have some concerns here.

3. Can Jane communicate effectively, both orally and in writing? While her basic understanding of the English language was good, she was not a great communicator. After reading her essays (which I'm not positive she wrote herself—more on this later), I don't feel I

understand who she is and where she's going. During the interview, she was stiff and had difficulty answering some basic questions. More concerns.

4. Does Jane demonstrate leadership skills or potential? Absolutely not. She has no relevant experiences, doesn't enjoy working in groups, and was not involved in any extracurricular activities as an undergraduate. None of her letters of recommendation mention leadership potential.

5. Does Jane conduct herself honorably and ethically? After the interview, I noticed a disconnect between her speaking style and the writing style conveyed in her essays. Her essays contained a lot of big words and complex ideas. In the interview, however, she preferred very brief answers. When I asked about some of the content in her essays, she had a hard time relaying some of the information she supposedly wrote. I'm now very suspicious that she did not write her own essays, which is a *huge* red flag. This not only makes me question her ethics but also makes me wonder if she will be able to succeed in her writing-intensive coursework.

6. Will Jane be a good team member? Would I want to work with her? This is a tough one. She was very nice and polite, and I know she is intelligent. Still, she said she prefers working alone to teamwork. None of her letters of recommendation indicate that she's a team player. That's a problem because most of our coursework is done in teams. Furthermore, most of our employers want to hire future leaders with exceptional interpersonal skills and a strong desire to work in teams.

7. Will Jane be employable by graduation? Would I hire her? Another tough one. For certain roles, she may

be a great fit. She has an engineering background and speaks three languages, so I'm sure she will find a job somewhere. But will the employers who typically recruit our MBA students be interested in her for a high-level management role? Maybe, but probably not.

> **Had our decision been based solely on her grades and test scores, Jane probably would have been admitted; however,** after a more holistic review, her application became much less competitive.

8. Does Jane specifically want to attend our school? Will she stay involved beyond graduation? There's no question that Jane wanted to attend our program. She spent time in both her essays and interview talking about how her dad went to our school and how her dream is to follow him there. Although we like passion for our program, we are more concerned with whether applicants are likely to stay involved beyond graduation. Will they open pipelines at their future employer to recruit at our school? Will they host recruiting events abroad for prospective students in their home country? Will they help mentor future students? Again, nothing in Jane's application or interview tells me she's in this for the long haul.

Had our decision been based solely on her grades and test scores, Jane probably would have been admitted; however, after a more holistic review, her application became much less competitive. Of the three applicants we admitted instead of Jane, none had a higher GMAT score, but all had better essays and letters of recommendation and performed better in the interview.

So, what can you learn from Jane? Let's look at each component of the application.

Once you have a **GMAT** score within the acceptable range for the programs you are considering, move on and focus on other parts of your application.

The GMAT

The GMAT is a very important part of the admissions process. While not a predictor of leadership skills, team orientation, or employability, GMAT scores are correlated positively with performance in MBA coursework, particularly in quantitative subjects. In addition, the average GMAT score of the incoming class plays a role in how a program is ranked. Every program has a certain range of acceptable GMAT scores. For some programs that score is 500; for others it's more than 700. Some schools have a broad range of acceptable scores, while others have a much narrower window. Some schools make the acceptable range easy to find by publishing their minimum required or average GMAT scores on their website. For other schools, you may have to talk with the admissions team during a recruiting event. Regardless, the key takeaway is this: Once you have a

GMAT score within the acceptable range for the programs you are considering, move on and focus on other parts of your application. Don't continue to take the exam, hoping a small increase in your score will increase your chances of admission. Jane chose to take the GMAT six times, and her score went up only forty points. Had she used that time to focus on her essays, secure strong letters of recommendation, and practice for the interview, the time better spent may have helped her achieve her goal.

Still don't believe you need to do more than score well on the GMAT to get in to a top program? Let's look at some numbers. According to *U.S. News & World Report*,[2] the total full-time enrollment of the Top Ten MBA programs in 2014 was 10,407 students. Given these are two-year MBA programs, only half the seats are available each year. In other words, there are about 5,204 slots available in the Top Ten programs each year.

Now, let's assume you get an awesome score on the GMAT—say a 700. Do you think this guarantees you a seat in a Top Ten program? Think again. According to the Graduate Management Admission Council (GMAC),[3] 243,529 GMATs were taken between July 1, 2013, and June 30, 2014. Of these, GMAC estimates eighty percent were taken by unique testers. The other twenty percent of scores are from the same person taking the exam more than once. That leaves us with 194,823 unique test takers. GMAC says an overall score of 700 is in the

---

2 "Best Business Schools," *U.S. News & World Report*, 2015, http://grad-schools. usnews.rankingsandreviews.com/best-graduate-schools/top-business-schools/ mba-rankings?int=9dc208.

3 http://www.gmac.com/frequently-asked-questions/application-trends-survey-benchmark-tool.aspx

eighty-ninth percentile,[4] meaning that eleven percent of all test takers (21,431 of the 194,823) scored at or above this level. (See the Appendix for a detailed breakdown of the figures used in this analysis.)

The GMAT score is important, but it is not the sole determinant of admissibility.

All of this means that more than 20,000 students are competing for about 5,000 seats in top programs. Now, for simplicity's sake, let's assume that the top programs admit only the best GMAT test takers. (This is not quite accurate—more on this later.) That means that three out of every four applicants with a 700 or higher GMAT score will *not* be admitted to a Top Ten program. Obviously, the GMAT score is important, but it is not the sole determinant of admissibility. This is as true with Top Ten programs as it is with Top One Hundred or unranked programs.

Of course, this is just a rough illustration, as the reality is more complicated. Even the best programs admit some students with low GMAT scores. In fact, at Stanford the GMAT range for this year's incoming class was from 550 to 790.[5] Also,

---

4   Graduate Management Admission Council, "GMAT Scoring by Exam Section/ GMAT Benchmarking Tool," 2016, http://www.gmac.com/gmat/learn-about-the-gmat-exam/gmat-scoring-by-exam-section-normal-view.aspx.

5   Stanford Graduate School of Business, "Entering Class Profile," October 8, 2015, https://www.gsb.stanford.edu/programs/mba/admission/evaluation-criteria/class-profile.

some applicants with top GMAT scores may not apply to a Top Ten program for a variety of reasons.

My point, however, is that a good score alone is not a guarantee of admission at any school. Your GMAT score is kind of like your ticket to the big dance—it gets you in the door but doesn't guarantee anyone is going to dance with you. Get yourself a ticket by scoring in the right range; then spend some time working on your dance moves.

Transcripts

Although you can't change the past, you can offset poor undergraduate grades by highlighting recent academic successes. For example, taking a math or undergraduate business course at a local community college may demonstrate your aptitude for business education. Highlighting professional certifications, especially those requiring an exam, also can help.

A few years ago, I had to deny an applicant I really liked, because his undergraduate grades were just too low to make him a viable candidate. He was very successful in his career, and I had no doubt he had the soft skills that we were looking for. As I gave him the bad news, I told him we couldn't move forward at this time, but I let him know the door was open if he could demonstrate his ability to succeed in an academic environment. A year later he reapplied after taking three math classes and an introductory accounting course at a local community college. His 4.0 GPA in these classes was more than enough to demonstrate his academic capabilities. Based on this new information, he was admitted to the program.

Other tips regarding transcripts include the following:

- Be sure to review your transcripts thoroughly before submitting them to any graduate program. If any of them contain incorrect information, it's much easier to resolve the issue with your undergraduate institution before applying for business school than after.

- Always include transcripts for all classes you have taken since completing your bachelor's degree. Even noncredit classes can help demonstrate an appreciation for learning and may enhance your application.

- If you studied in a non-English-speaking country, be sure to include officially translated copies of your transcripts in addition to the native-language version.

- Transcripts should always be sent directly from the conferring institution to the program you are applying to. In most schools, unofficial transcripts cannot be used to make an admissions decision.

Essays

As noted earlier, essays are an important component of the admissions process because they highlight applicants' ability to think and write clearly. They also help the admissions committee understand the applicants' rationale for wanting to earn an MBA as well as their postgraduation career and life plans. Here are some tips to help ensure your essays enhance your application:

- Write your own essays. Paying someone to write your essays for you is a terrible idea. Chances are that person has already written the same essays for countless other clients. When I see essays that are obviously plagiarized, it tells me the applicant is either lazy, lacks the written communication abilities required for success in the program, or both.

- That being said, it's a good idea to have a friend or family member review your essays checking for clarity, spelling, and grammar.

- Essays can be a great opportunity to discuss setbacks or weak spots in your application. One of the best essays I ever read was from an applicant who dreamed of becoming an entrepreneur but failed in her first endeavor because she lacked the business skills to successfully run the organization. She saw earning her MBA as a way to ensure her next company would be successful. Her essay was not only compelling but also explained the significant gaps in her work history that had raised a few eyebrows when reviewing her resume.

- Regardless of the specific essay question, try to weave the themes of ethics, teamwork, and leadership into your essays. Giving vivid examples that highlight these traits shows the admissions committee that you understand what the MBA is really about.

- Personalize each essay for the school to which you are applying. Try to add program-specific attributes, abbreviations, and examples as appropriate. Even if you don't follow this advice, please double-, triple-, and quadruple-check that you don't accidentally use the name of another program in your essays. It happens all the time, and it can be extremely detrimental to your chances.

Only a handful of essays have talked about what the applicants would contribute to our program.

- I've read thousands of essays, most of which articulated why an applicant was a good fit for our program. These essays tended to talk about how our program and alumni contacts would help the applicants get a job in a dream field. However, only a handful of essays have looked at the question from the other side and talked about what the applicants would *contribute* to our program. Articulating how your experiences, connections, and skills may benefit your fellow classmates and alumni is a good idea. Examples include industry connections that may be of interest to classmates, the desire to start a new student club, or an interest in serving as a student ambassador.

Letters of Recommendation

Generally speaking, your letters of recommendation (LOR) should come from academic or professional sources. Academic sources can include professors, advisors, and coaches. Professional sources may include supervisors, colleagues, or customers and clients. If you are involved with a religious organization or volunteer your time with a charitable enterprise, an LOR from a leader of that organization is perfectly acceptable. LOR should never come from friends or family.

So, what makes a good LOR?

DETAILS

Because most LOR are positive, it's the more detailed ones that are most useful. It's also helpful if the recommender outlines the applicant's specific skills or strengths and can support these assertions with details. For example, saying the applicant is a good manager is OK. Saying that the applicant managed a team of ten and a $50 million budget for five years—and that during that time sales grew by fifty percent while turnover was nearly nonexistent—is much more descriptive and therefore more helpful.

HONESTY

I once read an LOR stating that as an intern, the candidate developed and launched a new product that sold more than five million units in its first year on the market. This seemed very impressive, and I wanted to learn more. When attempting to contact the recommender, I learned that neither the company nor the recommender actually existed. While this is an extreme example (and one that did not end well for the applicant), applicants sometimes encourage their recommenders to bend the truth. Apart from the ethical questions this behavior raises, it actually detracts from the application. In fact, offering some areas for improvement adds credibility to the recommendation. No one is perfect, and when an LOR can make a strong case for how an applicant overcomes weaknesses, it signals to the admissions committee that he or she will do what it takes to be successful in an MBA program. On a related note, I appreciate recommenders' including their contact information and encouraging me to follow up with them for more information.

PERSPECTIVE

I like recommenders to introduce themselves and explicitly state their relationship to the applicant. Mentioning how long they have known the applicant provides some important context to the admissions committee. In addition, contrasting the applicant with other employees they have managed, students they have taught, or volunteers they have supervised helps illustrate the traits that make this applicant unique. For example, a letter from a professor who states the applicant took her class and earned a B is OK; however, a letter stating that of the thousands of students she's taught in her career, this applicant stands out because of his passion for the subject matter, work ethic, and presentation skills is extremely helpful to the admissions committee.

Here are some other tips for your LOR:

- LOR can be very helpful in addressing weaknesses in your application. For example, if you have limited work experience, having an LOR that describes how much you accomplished during your internship can be very helpful. If you have a lower GPA, an LOR from a professor confirming your academic and quantitative abilities will go a long way.

- Think holistically about LOR. If a school asks for three letters, it may make sense to have one from a boss or supervisor at your current company, one from a professor, and one from an organization where you volunteer your time. The one from your boss may focus on your impact at the organization, leadership skills, communication abilities, team orientation, and ability to multitask. The academic recommendation may illustrate your work ethic, quantitative and problem-solving abilities, and the pride you take in your work. The LOR from the organization with which you volunteer may offer examples of your desire to help others, unselfishness, leadership capabilities, and ability to connect with people.

- The quality of the relationship between the applicant and the recommender is much more important to the admissions committee than the title of the recommender. Avoid the temptation to ask the CEO and the dean for LOR unless they know you well enough to write a detailed letter. A memorable example of this was the student who submitted an LOR from President Obama. The applicant had worked on the president's reelection campaign, and the letter made it very clear that the president had never met this person. It was a generic form letter that could have been written for anyone. As a result, the letter did nothing to enhance the application.

> **Strong applicants who ace the interview enhance their scholarship opportunities, while those who appear weaker on paper can bolster their odds of admission with a strong interview.**

The Interview

I weight the interview very heavily when making an admissions recommendation or decision. It's a great opportunity for both parties to explore fit. Strong applicants who ace the interview enhance their scholarship opportunities, while those who appear weaker on paper can bolster their odds of admission with a strong interview. Here are some tips for a positive and productive interview.

BEFORE THE INTERVIEW

- Research the school and interviewer beforehand. It's OK to view the interviewer's LinkedIn profile, but don't cyberstalk—I once had an interviewee mention my wife and dog during the first five minutes of our conversation. I asked him about it, and he said he had checked out my Facebook profile. It came across as a little creepy. That being said, knowing what professional associations your interviewer belongs to and his or her alma mater and most recent former job may help you establish rapport during the interview.

- Ensure your social media pages showcase your personality and achievements in a professional manner. It's not uncommon for an interviewer to review an applicant's LinkedIn or Facebook page prior to an interview. I once viewed the Facebook profile of an applicant while I was interviewing him over Skype. As he was telling me about his professional accomplishments, his profile picture loaded on my screen. The image showed him at a bar, presumably very drunk, grabbing a girl's butt. While it didn't completely derail the interview, it gave me pause about his professionalism, maturity, and ability to relate to alumni and employers.

- Know the basics about the program, including terminology, names of specializations, building names, and so on. Taking the time to learn this information will demonstrate your sincere interest in the program to your interviewer. Conversely, mispronouncing the name of the school, talking about programs that don't exist, or accidently using the name of another program will damage your credibility. Don't laugh—it happens all the time.

- If you are going to conduct your interview over Skype, be sure to test your microphone and connection speed ahead of time. It's very frustrating when we can't understand an applicant or are unable to have a decent conversation because of technology issues. Also, make sure you take the call from a professional location. I once tried to interview a candidate while she was at a bar. While sipping on a martini, she told me she was meeting her friends there after the interview. Not only was it difficult for us to hear each other over the loud music and other conversations, but the applicant's choice of location also caused me to question how serious she was about attending our program.

- If you look hard enough in MBA chat rooms, you will find examples of prospective students posting the name of their interviewer and the exact questions they were asked. I highly recommend resisting the temptation to do this. Instead of scouring the Internet for the "answer key" to your interview, practice the art and science of interviewing until you feel comfortable making a strong case for admission regardless of the questions asked. Good interviewers will change their questions based on the applicant's qualifications and the flow of the conversation.

DURING THE INTERVIEW

- Be prompt and dress professionally (even if the interview will be via Skype). I once commenced a Skype interview but couldn't see the applicant. I asked him to turn on his camera (the whole point of using Skype is the ability to see the person you are talking to and thus have a more interactive discussion). After a few seconds, an image of him in his boxer shorts eating dinner flooded my screen. Let me just say that this happened more than five years and five hundred interviews ago, and I still remember it like it was yesterday. It is not a fond memory.

- Offer vivid examples of academic projects, work experience, leadership opportunities, and so on. It may be helpful to bring a portfolio of past academic and professional projects to the interview. A portfolio is particularly useful in situational interview questions. Instead of telling the interviewer about a time when you worked on a difficult project with a tight timeline, you can present concrete evidence of your experience.

- Be open and honest about any weak areas in your application. Again, there is no such thing as a perfect candidate, and I like it when people frankly discuss low grades, low test scores, or poor work history in a way that demonstrates that they learned from the experience.

- Ask thoughtful questions (not ones that can be answered online). I typically schedule thirty-minute admissions interviews. I plan for my questions to last about twenty minutes and like to have between five and ten minutes to answer the applicant's questions at the end. When people use that time to ask me how long the program is, how much it costs, or where we are located, it's not only a waste of my time, but it's also a lost opportunity to gain insights from an insider. Examples of better questions include the following:

› How would you describe the culture of your program?

› Can you provide an example of a student with a background similar to mine who successfully transitioned to the XYZ industry at your school? If so, would it be possible to speak with him or her?

› What traits do you most often see in your most successful students?

› How does your program define student success?

› What new specializations or courses are currently under development?

› What differentiates your program from others?

› Who are the three most successful recent alumni from your program, and where are they working?

• Don't ask a lot of questions about scholarships, assistantships, and financial aid just yet, just as you wouldn't negotiate salary before getting the job. Your goal right now is to make a strong case for admission to the program. There will be plenty of time to discuss funding after you are admitted. Focusing on scholarships at this stage may backfire. It can come across as arrogant to some interviewers. It may also demonstrate your intent to attend whichever program offers the most funding, as opposed to the one that is the best fit for you.

AFTER THE INTERVIEW

- Send a thank-you note. It's OK to use email, which is quicker and more likely to get to the interviewer. Be sure the note conveys appreciation for the interviewer's time, notes your interest in the program, and mentions something memorable (and positive) about yourself.

- Follow up on any items you promised during the interview. If you mentioned your blog during the interview, include the link in your thank-you note. If you recently received a promotion, send an updated resume that includes your new responsibilities.

Key Takeaways

Perfect candidates may be admitted to their program of choice even if their essays and letters of recommendation are not great. Poorly qualified candidates may be rejected even with a great application. Those in the middle will benefit greatly from using the application and interview to tell their story in a unique and genuine manner. We like applicants who are professional, have clearly defined career goals, and want to attend our school. We also place a lot of emphasis on soft skills, including leadership, teamwork, and ethics.

Activity

Ask a family member or friend to conduct a practice admissions interview with you. After providing some information on your top school of choice, ask your volunteer to pretend to be the admissions director at that school. Have your interviewer ask you the following questions:

1. Tell me a little about yourself, including the highlights of your academic and professional background.

2. Why is this the right time for you to earn your MBA?

3. Why is our program the best fit for you?

4. What are your postgraduation plans?

See how well your answers reflect the main themes discussed in this lesson. Be sure to go beyond simply answering each question, offering as many examples and details as possible.

Repeat this exercise, changing the interviewer each time. Keep doing practice interviews until you feel comfortable highlighting your unique traits and experiences, regardless of the questions asked or the personality of the interviewer.

Reflection Questions

1. What unique experiences, capabilities, or attributes do I possess? Examples may include—

   › Extensive work experience

   › Experience leading multicultural teams

   › Exceptional grades in a tough subject

   › Military experience

   › Demonstrated impact in professional, volunteer, and academic endeavors

   › Exceptional interpersonal skills

> › Experience working or living in another country or the ability to speak multiple languages

> › Industry-specific knowledge

> › Experience starting a company or working at a start-up

2. How can I combine my strategy (see Lesson 2) with these characteristics to develop a unique, highly differentiated application?

3. Does my application answer the questions listed in this lesson?

4. What are the weak areas in my application? How can I offset them?

5. Do the various components of my application (e.g., LOR, essays, personal statement, and resume) tell a unique, memorable, genuine, and consistent story?

6. How can I improve the student or alumni community of the schools I am considering? Have I demonstrated in my application the willingness to do this?

7. Have I incorporated program-specific information into my application?

8. Am I one hundred percent sure I didn't use the name of another school or program in my essays?

Now What?

In the next lesson, I'll help you navigate an important next step: negotiating for scholarships and financial aid at the schools to which you were admitted.

NEGOTIATE LIKE A PRO

Less than ten seconds after I hung up, my colleague's phone lit up like Times Square on New Year's Eve. I had just ended a very tense conversation, and I was a little frazzled. An admitted student—we'll call him Brett—called and demanded that our office manager connect him to the admissions director "immediately." Before I could even say hello, he had already launched into a tirade aimed at convincing me that his scholarship offer was too low. He ranted for about ten minutes, and each time I tried to ask a question, he just talked right over me. He told me that he knew we gave other students more money and insisted that he had more lucrative offers from "better" schools. He told me he would go to the dean if I didn't help him. When he finally paused long enough for me to get a word in, I told him I would review his request with our admissions committee and get back to him in a few days.

My colleague, who had been listening from across the hall, hesitated a second and then picked up the phone. I could tell immediately it was Brett calling back to rant at someone else. My colleague shot me a grin, motioned for me to join him in his office, and then pressed "speakerphone."

A few days later, "Jennifer," another admitted student, asked to meet with me. Although she was not our strongest candidate on paper, we loved her attitude and believed strongly in her potential to succeed in our program. She came to several recruiting events and impressed everyone she met. Her application was great, and her interview convinced us not only to admit her but also to offer some scholarship funding. When she arrived, however, Jennifer's tone had changed. I asked if everything was OK. She said that the day her admissions letter came was the best day of her life, but when she started crunching the numbers, she wasn't sure if she could attend our program. She pulled out a spreadsheet showing her budget, including student loans, her personal savings, and a loan from her parents. She was about $10,000 short. She asked if she could work during her time in the program, or if living on campus instead of getting an apartment would save her some money. She ended our conversation by asking if I had any tips or advice for her.

That afternoon, I looked at our scholarship budget and saw that we had about $20,000 in funding left for the year. We could have made both students happy by increasing each of their scholarships by $10,000, but we went in a different direction. Our admissions committee decided to offer $20,000 to Jennifer, and Brett received nothing. In the end, we voted to allocate our limited funds on the student we really wanted in the class.

Other than the GMAT, scholarship negotiations may be applicants' most dreaded part of the MBA-admissions process. Despite what some students tell me, it doesn't have to be adversarial or stressful, and it can actually enhance your relationship with the MBA program director or admissions director. The key is to know whether and when to negotiate and to approach the negotiation with the right expectations and the right attitude.

Should You Negotiate?

If you have been following the advice in this book, you've identified programs that meet your unique goals, made a good impression during the recruiting process, submitted a high-quality application, and left a great impression during the interview. If you have been successful on all of these fronts, you may already have received a nice scholarship package. If not, hopefully the positive impressions you have made with the admissions team, students, alumni, and faculty along the way will be helpful as you negotiate for additional funding.

Here are some situations in which it may make sense to negotiate for additional funding:

- Your grades, test scores, and work experience are significantly higher than the averages listed in the school's latest class profile.

- You have identified your top school but can't afford the tuition after exhausting all financial resources available to you—these include federal student loans, parental/ family loans, work sponsorships, and personal savings.

- You are an international student, and your grades and test scores are significantly higher than the aver- ages from your home country—many MBA programs struggle to recruit a diverse class with representation from a variety of countries. Information on the average GMAT scores by country can be found on the GMAC website. I recommend taking a look at the most recent *Application Trends Survey*[1] in deciding whether it makes sense for you to negotiate your scholarship offer.

- You are a well-qualified female or underrepresented minority candidate. Most business schools also struggle to recruit both women and students from underserved popu- lations. Those applicants with work experience and excel- lent interpersonal skills are in especially high demand.

- Since applying, you have retaken the GMAT and earned a higher score, received a promotion at work, earned a new certification, or have significantly enhanced your qualifications in some other way.

Here are some bad reasons to negotiate. These arguments are unlikely to be successful with most admissions officers.

- You would like to graduate without any debt. That's great. I'd like to own a Tesla, but that doesn't mean anyone is going to give me one for free (if by any chance

---

1   http://www.gmac.com/market-intelligence-and-research/gmac-surveys/
app-survey.aspx

you do know someone giving away Teslas, please let me know). In most situations, students should expect to pay for at least some portion of their MBA education. Occasionally, full scholarships are offered, but typically this is the exception rather than the rule.

- Your friend, a colleague, or someone who posted on an MBA job board got a better offer. Would you ask your boss for a raise just because your colleague got one, or would you try to demonstrate why the value you add to the organization justifies an increase in your salary? The same logic applies here.

- Another school offered you more funding. I once had a student come to me with his scholarship letter from another school. The tuition for the other school was three times higher than ours, and they offered him only $5,000 more than we did. When I mentioned that the cost to attend our program was more than $100,000 less, despite the smaller scholarship, the student said, "That shouldn't matter. I'm going to go where I get the most scholarship. It shows they are more interested in me than you are." (On that latter point, he may have been right.)

- You are not seriously considering the program but hope to use a larger offer from your "safety school" as leverage in negotiating with your top school of choice. I worked with a student once who was admitted to our program with a scholarship. He negotiated for additional funding, and we gave it to him. He then called to tell me he was going to a competing school. A few weeks later he called back to say he changed his mind and wanted to accept our offer. Apparently, his first-choice school rejected his hardball-negotiation tactics, and he could not afford the tuition there. Unfortunately for him, we had already allocated his scholarship to another student. As a general rule, if you ask for something in a negotiation and receive what you asked for, you should accept the agreement immediately. Negotiating for what you want and then walking away when you get it destroys your credibility.

- Someone told you that you shouldn't have to pay for your master's degree. While it's true that some master's programs in the social sciences, physical sciences, humanities, and engineering may offer top applicants a tuition waiver, graduate assistantship, or other form of tuition remission, this tends to be less common for MBA programs. Why? Master's and PhD students in the aforementioned disciplines often conduct and publish research or receive grants that offset the cost of their studies. MBA students don't typically conduct academic research or work on grant-funded experiments.

How Should I Handle the Scholarship Negotiation?

If you decide to negotiate for additional funding, here are some tips to make the process as comfortable and professional as possible.

Do

- Have realistic expectations. Many applicants go into the admissions process expecting a full scholarship and are disappointed with anything less. Many variables affect a scholarship allocation, and some of these depend on the applicant (e.g., grades, GPA, letters of recommendation, test scores, and interactions with the admission team). Other variables may have to do with the funding available in a particular academic year, the number of applicants, or the internal goals of the specific program. An MBA is a valuable degree with a well-documented return on investment.[2] Going in with the expectation that you are going to have to fund at least a portion of your education is a smart assumption.

- Communicate professionally and respectfully with all members of the MBA team. Most programs track all interactions with prospective students. Being respectful to all MBA staff (including student workers and reception staff) demonstrates a level of professionalism that can only help your scholarship negotiation. The converse is also true. A few years ago, we revoked our offer of admission and scholarship to an applicant who was verbally abusive to our office manager over the phone.

- Ask not what the school can do for you . . . In a scholarship negotiation, instead of just asking for more funding, you might better serve your interests by communicating how you intend to support the culture of the program and enhance the student learning community. For example, if you intend to get involved with student organizations, mention your interest in serving in a leadership role. If you have industry connections that may benefit other students, or if you have connections to other high-quality applicants, it makes sense to discuss them with the admissions director.

---

2   Matt Symonds, "The ROI of B-School—Reach, Opportunities and Income," *Forbes*, February 17, 2015, http://www.forbes.com/sites/mattsymonds/2015/02/17/the-roi-of-b-school-reach-opportunities-and-income/.

- Crunch the numbers. Before scheduling a conversation to discuss your scholarship, I recommend doing an analysis of the gaps that exist between the tuition of the program you are considering and all available sources of funding (e.g., loans, grants, family support, and savings). Knowing that number will help you negotiate more effectively. In addition, if the admissions director knows you have some skin in the game—that you're willing to exhaust all sources of funding before asking for additional assistance—it may increase your chances of a successful outcome.

- Try to schedule a direct conversation in person, or via Skype. A scholarship negotiation should be scheduled and done in person, if possible. This demonstrates respect for the admissions director's time and shows you are serious about the program. When a face-to-face meeting isn't possible, Skype is preferable to the phone because it allows you to maintain eye contact and check for nonverbal cues. Be sure to dress professionally for this meeting.

Don't

- Don't issue any ultimatums. When a student tells me he or she will attend my program only if given a full ride or if we match the scholarship offered by another school, it demonstrates a lack of maturity and professionalism. More important, it is almost never successful. A much better idea is to use some of the tactics listed previously to make a case for increased scholarship.

- Don't compare offers between schools or applicants. MBA programs are not perfect substitutes; therefore, comparing your offer from a competing program is not a recommended strategy. As a program director, I do have some discretion with scholarship allocations, and I'm going to use it to help those I believe are genuinely interested in our program and will contribute positively to our school's culture. If I feel like a student is going to pick his or her school based solely on a scholarship offer, I almost never take the bait.

- Don't discuss your offer with other prospective students. A scholarship offer is personal and should be treated as confidential. Just as it is not advised to compare salaries at work, discussing your scholarship offer with other prospective students is detrimental to all parties. Telling me that I should increase your scholarship because someone else received a better one doesn't hurt only you; it also has the potential to damage the other applicant's relationship with the admissions committee. Your argument for increased funding should be based on your own needs and unique qualifications.

- Don't burn any bridges. Even if the scholarship negotiation does not go well, remain cordial and professional with the admissions director. Why is this a good idea? A few years ago, I worked with a student whom I really liked, but I wasn't able to meet her scholarship requirements. Even though she attended another institution, we stayed in touch and connected on LinkedIn. Last year, she emailed me to see if I could introduce her to one of my connections. That introduction led to a full-time job opportunity for her.

Key Takeaways

Scholarship negotiation, if done for the right reasons in a professional manner with reasonable expectations and utilizing rational arguments to justify the increase, can be an effective strategy to lower the cost of your business-school education. By following the advice in previous lessons, you have put yourself in a position to maximize the negotiation, because you have demonstrated your value to the program and school.

Activity

Practice a scholarship negotiation with a friend or family member. Pick a school you are hoping to attend, and research the tuition cost, average scholarship allocation, and typical class profile. Using the tips in this lesson, develop a professional, fact-based case for a scholarship based on your individual merits.

Once you've completed this legwork, ask your friend to pretend to be the program director for your school of choice. Provide your friend with the same information you just compiled, and present your case. Be sure to ask for a specific amount, as opposed to asking for a scholarship or more funding than you already received. Then have your friend respond with some soft objections including the following:

- Based on your profile, we believe the scholarship you were already offered is very fair.

- We would love to offer you a scholarship, but we have no more funding for this academic year.

- We still have a large number of offers outstanding, so we can't offer additional funding at this time.

Think about how you will react to each of these common responses. If the objection is based on your profile, perhaps discussing some of your intangible qualities and how you intend to enhance the student learning community may be beneficial. If the program can't allocate additional funding this year, ask if a scholarship could be provided if you deferred your application a year. You may also ask if there are ways to earn additional funding, either by teaching an undergraduate class, grading papers for a professor, or working in the admissions office. In the third scenario, consider asking for an extension of your decision deadline to allow the program additional time to determine whether to increase your scholarship.

Keep practicing until you feel comfortable making your case and can easily respond to common objections.

Reflection Questions

1. Do I have a strong case for an increased scholarship based on my qualifications?

2. What are the desired outcomes of my scholarship negotiation?

3. In light of my qualifications versus the published class profile, are my expectations reasonable?

4. What rationale will I use to drive my scholarship negotiation? How can I support my case?

5. Can I demonstrate that I am invested in my education and have some "skin in the game"?

Now What?

Now that you have been admitted to one of your top programs with a nice scholarship, let's focus on some tips for maximizing your experience as a student in your chosen program. We will start by discussing a fairly common mistake—overemphasis on grades.

PART 2

GET CONNECTED

DO MORE THAN STUDY

No one was super-excited about the assignment. It was the end of MBA orientation, and everyone was looking forward to a relaxing weekend before classes started on Monday. At about 4:00 p.m. on Friday, we were placed into our project teams and given our first task. Little did I know this project would set the tone for my entire MBA-student experience.

The rules were simple enough. We were to take a popular song and change the words to reflect our thoughts on what being an MBA student would be like. We had until Monday morning to write the lyrics and prepare to sing our masterpiece to faculty and fellow students. The winning team, as determined by popular vote, would receive tickets to any show at the school's performing-arts center.

I didn't think we would win. There were certainly more clever entries, and many teams had considerably more musical talent. One group changed "I Want It That Way" by the Backstreet Boys to "I Want My MBA." Another team transformed Will Smith's "Welcome to Miami" into "Welcome to Urbana" (". . . party in the cornfields to the break of dawn . . ."). We went with a classic—morphing John, Paul, George, and Ringo's "Let It Be" into "Get a B." Our message was this: Do more than just study. Much to my surprise, we were a hit and won handily! During our live performance, most of our classmates and even some faculty joined in for the last chorus, which went something like "Get a B. Get a B, not a C, yeah. Get a B . . ."

Our lyrics were more prophetic than I knew at the time. I quickly learned that some of the most valuable and enduring learning experiences would happen outside the classroom. They would happen in China while I toured the Great Wall with my classmates. They would happen at case competitions when our team went up against students from top schools and came out on top. They would happen when some classmates and I decided to start a company. They would happen as I barely escaped death on a white-water rafting trip in New Zealand. They would also happen informally over a meal or at "Mugclub"—our Thursday evening social. The experiences I had during my MBA not only led to an exciting job in a new field, but they also transformed me into a better professional with a wider global outlook. While I appreciate the academic rigor of my education, I'm equally thankful for the opportunities I was given that transpired beyond the confines of the classroom.

As an MBA program director, I work with students all the time who underestimate the value of experiential learning. One memorable example was a student named "Tom" who dropped by my office about two months before graduation. Tom had earned all As in his classes but was struggling to connect with potential employers on job interviews. "I've had eight interviews in the last two weeks, but none chose to bring me on-site for a second-round interview," he lamented. I asked how he thought he was differentiating himself from others applying for the same job. Without hesitation, he said, "I have a 4.0 GPA. That should be enough." Instead of arguing or offering unsolicited theories about why his interviews weren't going well, I suggested he contact the people who interviewed him to ask for candid feedback. By the next week, he had gotten in touch with two of his interviewers. "One told me he really liked me, but the other candidates had better answers to her situational interview questions. The other said he won't hire anyone that can't demonstrate that they have had a positive impact on those around them." With that feedback in hand, Tom decided to make some changes to his job-search strategy.

His efforts paid off a few weeks later at an alumni reception in Chicago. He connected with an alumnus at one of the companies that had rejected him earlier. He followed up and asked if he could shadow this person to learn more about the company and the industry. Two interesting things happened that day. First, he was introduced to a hiring manager in a different division who agreed to interview him on the basis of the alumnus's recommendation. Second, by missing class to attend the job shadow, he missed a quiz, resulting in the first B of his MBA career. Tom didn't graduate with a 4.0, but he left with a job offer from a Fortune 100 company. Had he continued to put academics ahead of everything else, the reverse probably would have occurred.

It's not that grades aren't important. In fact, top firms in investment banking and management consulting typically require nearly perfect grades from the candidates they are even remotely considering hiring. Employers in many other industries are most interested in hiring well-rounded individuals with demonstrated leadership, managerial, and interpersonal skills.

Here are some ways to gain skills and experiences demanded by employers as an MBA student.

Case competitions offer a great opportunity for students to practice all of the skills that make an effective business leader.

Case Competitions

In a case competition, as you may recall, teams of business students compete to develop the best solution to a business problem, usually under intense time pressure. Teams are typically given about twenty-four hours to read and analyze a business case, conduct research utilizing all publicly available information, and develop findings and recommendations that they present to a panel of judges. The case usually focuses on a company about to make a critical decision, like entry into a new market, creation of a new product, or implementation of a new human resources policy. Participants need to identify the key issue of the case and analyze the variables from multiple perspectives. Prizes are often awarded to both the winning team and standout contributors from other teams.

I like case competitions for many reasons. They offer a great opportunity for students to practice all of the skills that make an effective business leader—teamwork, strategic analysis, research, presentation, and time management—in an intense but educationally oriented setting. Case competitions are also amazing networking opportunities. Often the judges and the sponsoring organizations use the opportunity to scout for top MBA talent. Several students I've worked with were offered interviews, internships, and even full-time jobs as a result of their participation in a case competition. Case competitions also provide participants with vivid examples to use in their answers to situational questions asked during job interviews. If you are interviewing for a manager position, chances are you will hear a prompt along the lines of this one: "Tell me about a time when you worked with a team to deliver high-quality results under time pressure." Participation in case competitions makes these types of questions a breeze to answer.

Study Abroad

Before starting my MBA program, I had traveled to Canada and Mexico but hadn't strayed beyond North America. That changed during the first year of my MBA program when I had the opportunity to study entrepreneurship in China over the winter break. For three weeks, we visited start-ups, well-established companies, universities, historic sites, and alumni in six different cities. Along the way, I learned about the history and culture of the Chinese people, talked about the paradox of an entrepreneurship culture existing in a traditionally government-controlled economy, sampled some amazing food, and met several extremely successful professionals. During my second year, our global-marketing professor took us on a fourteen-day adventure to his native New Zealand. We studied the wool industry, and used our findings to develop a U.S. market–entry strategy, which we presented to a local clothing manufacturer. Between tours of wool factories and meetings with high-level executives, we went skydiving, swam with the dolphins, stayed at a sheep farm, and narrowly defied death on a white-water rafting trip.

While extremely enjoyable, these trips were so much more than vacations. They were learning opportunities—opportunities to explore how a country's history and business culture intersect, chances to see the emergence of the innovation economy in one of the world's largest nations, and the ability to witness firsthand the differences in communication and negotiation styles in different parts of the world. These experiences have made me a better professional. I can now better relate to prospective and current students from China. I've tailored my oral and written communications as a result of what I learned in that country. These small changes haven't gone unnoticed. Just last year, a student from China told me she chose our school because I made her feel welcome during the interview process.

I believe international travel can benefit all students, and I highly recommend considering a study-abroad opportunity if any of these situations apply to you:

- You have not had the opportunity to travel outside of the United States.

- Several of the companies you are considering are headquartered outside the United States.

- You would like to live and work outside the United States (or your home country) after graduation.

- You want to demonstrate to a future employer your understanding of the global nature of business.

- You are interested in working for a multina-tional corporation upon graduation.

- You are interested in learning about other cultures.

Student Clubs and Organizations

Most programs have a wide variety of student clubs and organi-zations run by MBA students. Some clubs are industry specific (e.g., finance clubs, marketing clubs, consulting clubs), some are social or recreational (one of the schools I worked for had a wine club), and others focus on the needs of specific popula-tions of business students (e.g., clubs for women in business).

Each club typically has a leadership team responsible for fundraising, hosting events, organizing professional-development opportunities for their members, and market-ing their organization to fellow students, faculty, and alumni. Students are usually elected to leadership positions by their classmates. Many programs encourage students to create new organizations if there is demand from the student body.

Serving in an elected leadership role is a great experien-tial learning opportunity. Successfully leading an organization requires the same skills—ability to inspire others, communica-tion, fundraising, strategic planning, budgeting, and customer service—required to lead in the business world. Like studying abroad or participating in a case competition, the experience of leading a student organization not only enhances your skills but also provides anecdotes and experiences you can reference in job interviews to answer questions about leadership, teamwork, ability to drive results, and time management.

Experiential Projects, Classes, and Experiences

As an MBA student, I had the opportunity to participate in Illinois Business Consulting (IBC)[1], a for-profit management-consulting firm run by business students at the University of Illinois. Those with previous consulting experience served as the leadership team, which interfaced with clients and trained less experienced students. Projects ranged from helping a Fortune 100 company create a new product-development strategy in China to working with a local car wash looking for ways to attract new customers. Many of our clients were alumni with hiring authority in their respective organizations.

Because IBC is a mostly volunteer entity, the hours were long and the pay was (very) low, but the experiences I gained as a result of participating in IBC have helped me to this day. I learned how to develop, motivate, and train others; manage projects; and track expenditures to budgets. Most important, I learned the value of providing excellent customer service. Interestingly enough, the job-placement rate for students in my graduating class who chose to participate in IBC was one hundred percent. Almost all of us had multiple offers.

I recommend taking advantage of any coursework or IBC-like experiences that allow you to work on real projects sponsored by real potential employers. Whether it's developing a financial model for a huge corporation, helping the local

---

1   http://www.ibc.illinois.edu/

bakery streamline its operations, or working with a regional nonprofit to more thoroughly engage its donor base, something powerful happens when MBA coursework is applied in a real-world context. Such projects reinforce concepts learned in the classroom, but more important, they provide students—particularly those with limited work experience—the ability to showcase their problem-solving, managerial, leadership, and interpersonal skills to future employers.

Volunteering your time with a start-up company that interests you can be a win-win situation.

Working with Start-Ups

Many universities, particularly large research-oriented universities, actively commercialize the technologies created in labs on campus. There are many reasons to do this, including enhancing the university's reputation, financial incentives, and the intrinsic value of bringing to the marketplace products that improve the quality of life for all. For example, the first magnetic resonance imaging (MRI) machine, light-emitting diode (LED), and web browser (Mosaic) were all developed at the University of Illinois.[2]

Why is this relevant to you? Because start-up companies, particularly those focused on commercializing new technologies,

---

2 University of Illinois, "Research Milestones," 2015, http://illinois.edu/about/research.html.

need business expertise to improve their likelihood of success. They need professionals who can help them identify the best markets for their new products, analyze competitors, develop a marketing plan, interface with customers and partners, manage cash flow (in start-ups, cash is very limited, so this skill is especially beneficial), and facilitate the day-to-day operations of the new enterprise. Volunteering your time with a start-up company that interests you can be a win-win situation. The skills you are learning in class and through extracurricular activities will help the company prosper while the experiences you gain in the process will propel your career forward. In my experience, however, relationships between the companies in a university incubator or research park and the MBA program are not always formalized. Early stage start-ups are sometimes so focused on the technology that their leaders don't even think about the business they are trying to create. Often, MBA students have to take the initiative to connect with entrepreneurs and incubator staff. Students willing to take this extra step are often rewarded with some very interesting opportunities.

My first post-MBA job was with a start-up founded by electrical-engineering professors at the University of Illinois. It was one of the most challenging and exciting jobs I've ever had. The opportunity came about as a result of my summer internship at the university research park. I met the CEO of my eventual employer at a networking event at the university's incubator for tech start-ups. We hit it off, and I wound up doing some consulting work for him during my second year in the MBA program. Upon graduation, he offered me my dream job as the director of marketing. For the next five or more years, we worked together to transform a three-employee company with limited funding into a venture capital–funded entity with more than fifty employees, several product lines, and a viable customer base. This transformational and mutually beneficial experience solidified my belief in the importance of seeking out extracurricular learning opportunities in your areas of interest.

Key Takeaways

In this chapter, we examined overreliance on grades, another typical mistake made by some MBA students. Although grades are important, employers of MBA students typically look for well-rounded individuals with demonstrated managerial, leadership, and interpersonal skills. Throughout this lesson, we discussed opportunities to enhance your abilities in these areas through experiential learning, or learning by doing.

Activity

Talk with at least ten MBA students who are in their second year or are recent graduates of your program. Ask them about their most significant moments in the program. Which activities were most beneficial to them? What do they wish they spent more time doing? What do they wish they spent less time doing? What advice do they have for a student just starting the MBA experience?

Reflection Questions

1. As an MBA student, how will I prioritize my time between academics, personal and professional development activities, and my career search?

2. What experiences as an MBA student will better prepare me for my chosen career?

3. Where can I gain these experiences while in business school?

4. Am I planning to study abroad? If so, have I factored the cost of a study abroad trip into my overall budget?

5. How important are grades in securing a job in my chosen industry? If I don't already know, how can I find out?

6. What unique, noncurricular opportunities exist at the programs I am considering?

7. What will my legacy as an MBA student be? Ten years from now, how will my classmates and faculty remember me?

Now What?

Now that we have talked about what to do in business school, let's switch gears and briefly talk about what not to do. In the next lesson, we will discuss academic dishonesty—a large and often unreported problem in modern business schools.

DON'T CHEAT

"It's just a coincidence," said "Gavin," scanning my face for a reaction. "We worked on that assignment all weekend." I tried unsuccessfully not to roll my eyes. In my left hand I was holding Gavin's team homework assignment on capital markets. In my right hand was a printout from Wikipedia on capital markets. The only difference between the two documents was the font.

Eventually, Gavin confessed that he had forgotten about the assignment until ten minutes before it was due. "I knew it was wrong," he fretted, "but I didn't want the entire team to fail because of my mistake." Unfortunately for Gavin (and his teammates), cheating didn't help them avoid that outcome. Gavin was handed an F for the course and his teammates earned a zero for the assignment. As a result, Gavin had to repeat the class and did not graduate with his classmates. More important, cheating cost him his future job. Gavin's offer at a leading consulting firm was rescinded when they learned why he would not be graduating with his cohort.

Sadly, in more than six years in academia, there hasn't been a single semester I haven't had to deal with at least one academic-dishonesty situation. Some have been completely accidental, and others have been even more willfully egregious than Gavin's example. The one common thread is that they were all completely avoidable. In this lesson, we will discuss academic dishonesty in detail. We will talk about its various forms, possible repercussions, and tips for staying on the right side of your program's honor code.

Types of Academic Dishonesty

Academic dishonesty comes in all different shapes and sizes. Following are some of the more common as well as some of the more elaborate forms I've witnessed.[1]

CHEATING

Cheating is a broad term that encompasses many dishonest acts, including—

- Acquiring an unauthorized advance copy of a test

---

1   DePauw University does a great job of defining several forms of academic dishonesty. I used some of DePauw's definitions and added some examples and anecdotes from my personal experience; DePauw University, "Types of Academic Dishonesty," 2016, http://www.depauw.edu/handbooks/academic/policies/integrity/types/.

- Using prohibited materials, such as an answer key, during an exam (this also includes using cell phones, calculators, or other electronic devices when not permitted by the professor)

- Glancing at another's test during an exam

- Presenting another student's homework, lab results, or other assignment as your own

- Lying to extend a deadline or cover up for a missed assignment

- Modifying graded material then resubmitting it and asking the teacher to correct the "error"

- Collaborating on individual assignments.

MBA programs are starting to crack down on cheating, particularly during quizzes and exams. Don't be surprised if your exam room has cameras or if multiple proctors are present during finals and midterms. One of the more egregious examples of cheating I've ever witnessed involved an MBA student breaking into a professor's office to steal a copy of an upcoming exam. He might have gotten away with his nefarious plan if he had bothered to steal the right test. Instead, he "borrowed" the undergraduate version of the test, which had different essay questions. When taking the real test, he wrote the answers to the undergraduate essays, which gave him away. Not only was he expelled from the program, but he was also arrested for breaking and entering.

FACILITATION

Cheating's close cousin is facilitation. Facilitation is purposely allowing or helping another student cheat. Examples of facilitation include

- Letting another student copy answers from your exam
- Taking an exam for another student
- Giving lab or simulation results to another student when not permitted by the professor to do so
- Providing your work to another student to copy
- Signing the attendance sheet for a classmate

If you think the consequences for facilitation are less severe, since the facilitator isn't the one doing the cheating, think again. If you knowingly allow someone to pass your work off as their own, you most likely will face the same consequences as the cheater. Sadly, this happened to one of my favorite students a few years ago. A caring person, she was concerned about a teammate on academic probation who was one C away from being dismissed from the program. She provided a copy of her statistics project to him so that he could "see my methodology for setting up the problem set." Unfortunately for her, the lazy student turned her work in as his own. He was caught because the professor was suspicious about his sudden artful mastery of the subject matter so soon after he had failed the midterm. Both students received a zero on the project. While her heart was in the right place, a far better strategy would have been for her to encourage the student to attend office hours, request outside tutoring, or speak with his academic advisor about his performance in class.

PLAGIARISM

Plagiarism is the act of taking another author's words or ideas without properly citing his or her work. Examples include—

- Copying information directly from a book, academic journal, magazine, the Internet, or other source without crediting the author

- Improperly citing a source in a paper, project, or other assignment

- Knowingly attributing information to the wrong source

- Falsifying quotations

- Falsifying a bibliography

Not all plagiarism is as egregious and intentional as Gavin's, which you read about at the beginning of the lesson. Plagiarism sometimes trips up students who aren't intentionally trying to cheat. For example, some students don't know when they have to cite sources or don't know how to cite them properly. As an MBA student, I was one of them. While doing market research for a project, I included the URL from an industry research website in my write-up, but I did not cite the source in the proper format. There was no intent to cheat, but my mistake earned me a lecture from the professor and a lower grade on the project.

A great resource for preventing accidental plagiarism is the Purdue University Online Writing Lab (OWL) (https://owl.english.purdue.edu/). This free tool offers instruction on how and when to cite sources and outlines specific steps to avoid plagiarism. In addition to the OWL, you can consult an academic-writing center. Available at most universities, these centers provide interested students with instruction on writing and offer proofreading and help with the citation process.

To combat plagiarism, more and more programs are using detection software like SafeAssign[2] and Turnitin.[3] These tools compare the content of a student's assignments to information published on the Internet, in academic journals, and in other classes and sections within the university. Programs utilizing plagiarism-detection software will require students to submit all papers, projects, and assignments electronically via the software manufacturer's platform. The work is scanned, and suspicious assignments are flagged for follow-up by the professor or teaching assistant. In my experience, both of these products do an excellent job of identifying potentially plagiarized material.

MISREPRESENTATION

Misrepresentation is lying about your academic credentials. It can include—

- Submitting MBA-application essays written by someone else

- Submitting letters of recommendation from people you haven't worked with (or who don't exist)

- Falsifying undergraduate transcripts or official test scores

Some students who misrepresent themselves on their MBA application believe that once they are admitted, they can't be punished if their transgressions are discovered. Wrong! I know personally of people who have been dismissed from their MBA

---

2   http://www.safeassign.com/

3   http://turnitin.com/

program because of irregularities discovered on their application after they were admitted.

DESTRUCTION OF MATERIALS

Every now and then I'll come across a special breed of cheater who goes beyond the ordinary tactics of copying others' work, preparing a cheat sheet for an exam, or copying content from the Internet. Not only do these students want to use unethical means to give themselves an advantage, but they also want to hurt their classmates in the process. We call this type of cheating destruction of materials. Examples may include—

- Stealing or destroying required course materials from the library

- Damaging public copies of textbooks or case packets

- Stealing or damaging required software on lab equipment (in the case of business school, some programs have computer labs with financial simulation software, market-research databases, etc.)

- Breaking into another classmate's computer to erase or modify his or her assignments

- Breaking into a professor's computer to change grades or steal assignments or tests

- Deliberately infecting the campus network with computer viruses

Students who get caught engaging in this type of behavior are usually dismissed from the program and may face legal consequences, depending on the value of the damaged property. In extreme cases, this type of cheating can result in a trip to the slammer. In 2014, a former Purdue student was sentenced to ninety days in jail for breaking into his professor's computer to change grades.[4]

Consequences

Depending on the severity of the incident and the number of previous academic-dishonesty situations a student has been involved in, consequences can range greatly. If you are found guilty of an academic-dishonesty charge, you may face one or more of the following:

- Verbal warning

- Written warning

- Grade of F for the assignment/test

- Grade of zero for the assignment/test

- Grade of F for the course

- Required attendance at an academic integrity workshop, which typically occurs on the weekend and requires the completion of a lengthy essay outlining your under-standing of the university's academic integrity policies

- Forfeiture of your scholarship

- Loss of your job as a student worker, teaching assistant, or graduate assistant

- Suspension from the program

- Expulsion from the program

- Arrest and prosecution

---

4   Allie Hastings, "Former Purdue Students Sentenced for Hacking, Changing Grades," *The Exponent*, February 28, 2014, http://www.purdueexponent.org/city_state/article_0b4ecb72-8135-54c3-8598-8b44cd90b7d4.html.

Unlike in our legal system, in an academic-dishonesty situation the burden of proof falls on the student.

Avoiding Academic-Dishonesty Situations

Even if you aren't found guilty, going through an academic-dishonesty investigation is time-consuming and stressful for the student (not to mention the faculty and administrative staff). It's also important to note that unlike in our legal system, in an academic-dishonesty situation the burden of proof falls on the student. In other words, the accused student must prove that he or she is innocent, rather than the accuser proving that the student is guilty. It's much easier to avoid the situation up front than to have to defend yourself if accused. Here are some tips for avoiding the situation:

- When in doubt about whether an assignment is team-based or individual, always ask the professor.

- If you forget about an assignment, communicate with the professor and ask for an extension. Even if your request isn't granted, it's better than the alternative. A failing grade on one assignment won't end your academic career, but cheating or plagiarism could.

- If you are having trouble in class, be sure to communicate with the professor. Try attending your professor's office hours or asking if you can meet to review key concepts.

- Keep your academic advisor informed if you are struggling with your coursework. Advisors can connect you with resources (e.g., tutors, academic-success centers, and writing professionals) to facilitate your studies.

- Understand that all group members are collectively responsible for group assignments. If one group member commits plagiarism, the whole group may be held accountable. Therefore, try to review all team assignments personally before they are turned in.

- If your program has an honor code, be sure to thoroughly read and understand the policy.

- If you have any doubts about how to properly cite sources, visit your campus library or academic-writing center.

- If your program utilizes plagiarism-detection software like Turnitin or SafeAssign, ask if students are allowed to proactively utilize the software to prevent accidental plagiarism. If so, download a copy and check all of your papers and assignments for unintentional mistakes before submitting final versions.

- If you witness cheating on assignments, projects, or exams, report it to the appropriate faculty member or program administrator. I know this is a tough one. It's much easier to turn a blind eye, but doing so only allows the cheating to continue. Eventually, students who don't cheat pay the price when their dishonest classmates earn higher grades on tests and assignments.

Cheating Really Doesn't Pay

Even if you get away with it once (or even more than once), cheating will catch up with you in the long run. One of the key themes of this book is that a major benefit of the MBA is the network you build as a student. That network can lead to job opportunities, business partnerships, new customers, and lifelong friendships. When you cheat, you decay that network. You create resentment (I worked really hard on that assignment and only earned a B, but you cheated and got an A); you lose the trust of your fellow students; and you lose the respect of faculty and staff. As we saw with Gavin's case, cheating can also hurt your reputation with employers or even cost you a job or internship opportunity.

One final thought: From what I've seen, academic dishonesty is far too prevalent in business schools. The only way to stop it is for students to understand what constitutes cheating, take a stand against it, and report incidents as soon as they occur. Remember, the reputation of your own degree hinges on the culture that you help create as a member of your program.

Key Takeaways

Academic dishonesty takes many different forms. In all cases, it is the student's responsibility to understand the rules and comply with them. The consequences of being found guilty of academic dishonesty range from embarrassing to catastrophic. Left unchecked, cheating can ruin the culture of a program. Most cases of academic dishonesty are entirely preventable.

Activity

Set up an appointment with your university's writing or academic-success center. Ask what resources exist to help students avoid accidental plagiarism.

Reflection Questions

1. What will I do if I find myself in a situation where I am unable to complete an assignment?

2. What will I do if I'm having trouble understanding the key concepts in a class?

3. What will I do if I find myself unprepared for an exam?

4. Do I understand my program's honor code? If my program doesn't have one, should I take the lead in creating one? (This is a great talking point with future employers.)

5. Do I know how to properly cite sources? If not, do I know where I can get help?

6. What will I do if I'm asked to help a classmate cheat on a project or an exam?

7. What will I do if I discover one of my teammates is turning in plagiarized work?

8. What resources are available to help me cope with stress?

9. What resources exist to help prevent cases of accidental plagiarism?

Now What?

I know you won't cheat in business school, so let's move on to another area in which some students struggle. In the next lesson, we will discuss another common mistake—overreliance on career services in your job search.

PART 3

GET HIRED

GO BEYOND CAREER SERVICES

It was a beautiful May afternoon. The sun was shining, and from my office window I could see dozens of events staff setting up for graduation that weekend. Campus was abuzz with excitement, particularly among our graduating second-year students.

I headed out for an afternoon coffee and ran into one of these soon-to-be graduates—let's call her Jennifer. "Hey, Jennifer." I casually waved as she passed. "Getting excited about graduation?" I asked, expecting the typical exuberant yes that I'd heard from so many others.

So, I was more than a little surprised by her terse response: "Not really." I detected both sadness and resentment in her voice.

I asked Jennifer to join me for coffee, during which she painted me a dismal picture of her postgraduation plans. "I'm graduating on Sunday, and I don't have a job. Career services completely failed me. None of the companies that came to campus were of interest to me. They didn't offer any help with other companies I was interested in working with. Now I have to face my parents and tell them I'll be moving back in with them."

Wanting to learn more, I asked a few follow-up questions. "How many times did you meet with career services?" (Twice.) "When did you start your job search?" (About a month ago.) "What resources besides career services did you use to facilitate your job search?" (None; I figured it was their job to ensure I was employed at graduation.)

Luckily for Jennifer, her story ultimately has a happy ending. Although she did have to crash in the parents' basement for a few months, she eventually landed a job as a financial analyst. (I should mention that she got the job through one of her classmates— more on the importance of leveraging your alumni network in the next chapter.) Although the story ended well, I believe Jennifer missed a key takeaway. She believed that the responsibility for her job placement rested with someone other than herself. I've seen this unfortunate mistake repeated by scores of MBA students each year. While most business schools invest vast resources in the professional development of their students, it is ultimately up to students to use those resources to meet their professional goals. In this lesson, we will discuss some strategies for doing this effectively.

What Is Career Services, and What Does It Do?

Most full-time MBA programs have a dedicated career-services team. Their responsibilities are multifaceted but generally fall under the umbrella of preparing students to compete for MBA-level jobs and connecting students with employers and professional-development resources. Most MBA career-services offices offer the following services:

- Resume reviews

- Mock interviews

- Help with cover letters

- Creation of a resume book that is disseminated to employers and alumni

- Communication about which companies will be conducting interviews on campus

- Individual career coaching

- Reporting on placement statistics for each MBA class

- Advising on salary negotiation

- Introductions to alumni at companies of interest to the student

Some career-services offices go beyond the basics and offer even more services, including:

- Executive coaching

- Professional-development classes and workshops

- Alumni mentoring programs

In addition to their student-interfacing responsibilities, most career-services departments dedicate resources to industry relations. Industry-relations professionals meet with alumni, employers, and other friends of the college to promote the achievements of the student body. From these conversations, industry-relations staff provide the faculty and program director with information about the skills and attributes most in demand in the marketplace.

Most career-services departments are more than willing to meet individually with interested students to develop a robust job-search strategy. In my experience, it is usually up to the student to initiate these conversations.

How Should You Use Career Services?

The career-services office can be an extremely helpful resource to utilize when conducting your job search. Here are some tips to maximize the benefit it can provide you.

Do

- Start working with career services as early as possible. It's not too early to start the summer before classes begin. If possible, email the career-services department, introduce yourself, and briefly state your postgraduation goals. Ask to meet, either in person or via Skype, that summer so you can hit the ground running in the fall.

- Be extremely professional in all of your interactions with career services. Showing up on time, communicating respectfully, and dressing appropriately

demonstrate maturity and professionalism, which
will benefit you if an alumnus or employer asks
about the program's standout students.

- Take advantage of every professional-development opportunity you are offered. Even if you feel overwhelmed with
classwork, make sure to attend all resume workshops,
company information sessions, mock interviews, and
professional-development seminars. In addition to gaining valuable insights, seizing professional-development
opportunities also demonstrates to the career-services
team that you are serious about your job search.

- Attend as many company informational sessions as possible, even if you aren't specifically targeting that company.
Again, this provides an opportunity to enhance your network and demonstrates your interest in your job search.

- Meet with your career-services contact at least once a
semester to touch base on your job search. Staying top
of mind is helpful to both you and your career-services
team, who have to remember professional and personal
details about dozens—if not hundreds—of other students.

- If you have contacts in industries of interest to your
classmates, share this information with career services
and offer to make an introduction to your colleagues.
This will show the career-services team that you are willing to contribute to the program, which will make them
more invested in helping you with your own job search.

- After developing a relationship over time with the career-
services team, politely ask for introductions to alumni
and employers in companies and industries of interest.

If you are unable to find what you are looking for from career services, check LinkedIn. You should be able to search for alumni of your program either at a specific company or in the industry most of interest to you.

Don't

- Don't wait until the last minute to start your job search. It can take a year or more of successful networking to find the right opportunity. If possible, start the summer before classes begin and dedicate time each week to professional networking, attending professional-development events, and meeting with alumni and recruiters. A classmate of mine (who successfully landed a great gig) adopted an interesting approach to time management. He told me he spent about one-third of his time on academics; one-third on his job search, professional development, and networking; and one-third sleeping, relaxing, and socializing with classmates.

- Don't walk into the career-services office and say, "I need a job." A general statement like that makes you look unfocused and unprofessional. Rather, spend some time identifying companies and industries of focus. Then put a plan together to learn as much about those companies and industries as possible. Once that plan is documented, meet with career services to get help enhancing the plan or filling in any gaps.

- Don't blow off a job interview or show up late. This is probably the number one way to get on the bad side of the career-services team. By not showing up for a scheduled interview, you hurt the reputation of the program and damage the credibility the industry-relations team has built with the company.

- Don't imply, either directly or indirectly, that your career-services contact is responsible for finding you a job. The career-services office is there to help, but at the end of the day, it is your responsibility to develop and execute your job-search strategy. In my experience, the difference between successful and unsuccessful job searches is the initiative taken by the student.

Going beyond Career Services

Although career services is an important resource, your job-search strategy should span well beyond the placement office. Here are some tips for going beyond career services to maximize your job search:

- Network, network, network (but do it well). Despite what I see all too often, networking is *not* calling or emailing an alumnus and asking for a job. It is about developing a mutually beneficial relationship over time. Good networkers go beyond their comfort zone and positively interact with everyone they meet. While they may be looking for ways to leverage the relationship for their benefit, they are also looking for opportunities to add value to the person they are meeting with. Successful networkers show genuine interest in others and give more than they take from their network. At a minimum, I'd recommend getting to know each of your classmates, faculty, and program staff during your time as a student. In learning about them, you may discover they have connections that may benefit you . . . and vice versa.

- If your school doesn't have a formal relationship with a company you are interested in, see if any alumni work there. If so, I recommend contacting them and asking if they would be willing to meet with you to discuss the company and industry. (Notice I did not say to call them and ask for a job.) If you do meet with an alumnus and that conversation goes well, I recommend asking if you could shadow him or her for a day at work. After a successful job shadow, it may be appropriate to ask for tips on job openings and interview strategies or introductions to hiring managers. One of my favorite examples of this was a friend of mine whose dream company was an elite management-consulting firm that did not recruit at our school. "John" reached out to an employee of the firm who had completed his undergraduate studies at our school and went on to earn his MBA from an elite program. The alumnus was able to connect John with a hiring manager who told him that despite his qualifications, the firm doesn't hire from "second-tier schools." Unfazed by this arrogant response, John replied, "Then don't hire me. I'll work for free." John's persistence and confident attitude impressed the hiring manager, who reluctantly offered him a summer internship (with pay). He had a great summer and earned a full-time offer upon graduation. Ten years later, after making partner, John left the firm to start his own company. I love John's (one hundred percent true) story because it illustrates the importance of networking and owning your job search and how persistence and the right attitude can open doors closed to those who sit back and wait for career services to find them a job.

- Develop an active, yet professional, social media presence. In addition to having an up-to-date LinkedIn profile, you may find it helpful to blog about some of the classes or projects relevant to the companies and industries you are pursuing. One memorable example of this was a student who did a live video blog at a case competition she attended. A few weeks later, the company who sponsored the case competition contacted her to schedule an interview for a role in their digital-marketing department.

- In some programs, full- and part-time MBA students are not in class at the same time and therefore have limited opportunities to get to know one another. Some programs offer executive MBA programs in a venue separate from the main campus. If possible, try to meet your classmates in other programs, particularly those in which most students are working full-time. This can be another source for job leads, introductions to employers, and advance notices of job postings.

A Final Thought

As an MBA student, you'll constantly be making choices about where to invest your time and energy. Often, professional development gets put on the back burner in favor of more immediate, pressing deadlines. When I was an MBA student, I once failed an assignment because I had an opportunity to interview with a company for an internship. I decided it was worth it to "Get a B" in that course because the interview led to an outstanding professional opportunity. Ultimately this decision helped my career more than an extra point on my final

GPA. Coursework, extracurricular activities, and other commitments can be overwhelming, but it is so important to consistently and regularly dedicate time and effort toward your job search.

Students who combine working with career services with proper networking and innovative social media marketing are more likely to land their dream job.

Key Takeaways

Career services is an invaluable resource as you search for your first post-MBA position. If you put in the time to develop a strong, professional relationship with career-services staff, they can help polish your resume, sharpen your interview skills, connect you with employers, and introduce you to alumni in your chosen industry. Ultimately, though, career services is not responsible for finding you a job—you are. It is up to you to define what success looks like and to develop a plan to get you there. Students who combine working with career services with proper networking and innovative social media marketing are more likely to land their dream job. Anything less and you'll put serious limits on your own job prospects or even end up like Jennifer—unemployed at graduation.

Activity

Prepare for a productive first meeting with your career-services representative. Create your resume and cover letters and identify specific industries and companies of interest. Then think about the skills and experiences desired by those organizations. Often you can ascertain this information by reading job descriptions on the company website or by reviewing the U.S. Bureau of Labor Statistics *Occupational Outlook Handbook*[1] for industry-specific information. Then develop a plan to gain the needed experiences and skills during your MBA program. For example, if you are seeking a management role upon graduation, serving as the president of a student club may demonstrate that you have the leadership skills and drive required for success.

Once you have created and documented your plan, meet with your career-services representative. Review your plan with the representative, asking for suggestions for improvement. Ask for introductions to alumni or second-year students who have successfully found employment or internship opportunities in your desired field. Determine which companies that already have a formal relationship with the university are hiring in your desired field and when they will be on campus. Ask for introductions to hiring managers and other key alumni at the company or within the industries of interest. Be sure to follow up on everything suggested by your career-services representative and send a quick thank-you note.

---

1   http://www.bls.gov/ooh/

Reflection Questions

1. When should I start my job search?

2. How will I ensure I'm dedicating time to my job search each week?

3. Which faculty and program staff may be most helpful in my job search? How can I start building a relationship with them?

4. How will I effectively utilize career services in my search?

5. What resources besides career services will I utilize in my job search?

Now What?

Now that you understand the importance of owning your career search, let's talk about what happens after you land your dream job. In the next lesson, we will discuss one of the most common mistakes I witness—failure to stay connected as an alumnus. We will look at how this mistake negatively affects both the program and the alumnus.

UTILIZE AND NOURISH YOUR ALUMNI NETWORK

TO: Greg@WidgetCo.com
FROM: brian.precious@university.edu
DATE: October 5, 2011
SUBJECT: Congratulations on your new job!

Hi Greg,

I just saw on LinkedIn you started a new job at WidgetCo. Congrats! You worked really hard in school and I'm happy to hear you've landed this great position.

I'd love to hear more about your role and experiences to date. We have several students interested in employment opportunities there. Can we chat when you get settled?

Best,
Brian Precious

TO: brian.precious@university.edu
FROM: Greg@WidgetCo.com
DATE: November 6, 2011
SUBJECT: RE: Congratulations on your new job!

Brian,
I'm way too busy to meet about this right now. — Greg

Although slightly annoyed, I wasn't altogether surprised by Greg's terse reply to my request. He was an extremely bright and generally nice guy, but he never really understood the importance of maintaining his professional network. He attributed his career successes to his own actions and didn't seem to be blessed with the "pay it forward" gene.

I didn't think about Greg again until about two years later when he emailed me out of the blue. He wanted to let me know he'd been laid off and asked if I could help him with his job search. Although I wasn't left with a great impression after our last interaction, I agreed to meet him for lunch and suggested he reach out to a few of his classmates. However, for each student I mentioned, Greg gave another reason that he wasn't going to reach out. I tried offering names of a few alumni that might be of assistance, but he showed no interest in contacting them either. I left the meeting feeling I had wasted my time.

Greg eventually found another job on his own, though he certainly would have opened up more options if he had followed up with even a few of my suggestions. Years later, I reached out to him again, asking if he would be willing to meet with an especially gifted prospective student who was hoping to work at Greg's new company. To this day, I still haven't heard back from Greg. (Luckily, the prospective student chose our program and wound up having a great experience.)

Greg is an egregious example of an all-too-common trap into which some MBA graduates fall: failure to give back to the network after graduation. Staying connected with classmates, faculty, and program staff has many advantages for both the alumnus and the program. In this lesson, we will discuss these advantages and offer some suggestions for how to stay connected.

Why Stay Connected?

Staying involved with your program can be extremely advantageous to you. Here are some actual examples of the benefits I've witnessed with recent alumni:

- A few years after graduation, Susan's company asked her to relocate to Hong Kong. Susan reached out to her classmates that lived there, and they helped her find housing and complete the necessary employment paperwork. They even allowed her to stay with them for two weeks before her apartment was ready. By the time she started her new position, she was practically a local.

- Tim was laid off a few years after graduation from his MBA program. Through a relationship with one of his classmates, he was connected to a local start-up that was eventually acquired by a major software company. He now works in a leadership position for a Fortune 100 company.

- In my role as program director, I was asked to organize a recruiting event in South Korea. I reached out to my MBA classmates there, who were excited to help. They secured a room for our event and found a local company to sponsor our visit. They even connected us with local government officials responsible for awarding scholarships to top students in-country.

- Tina decided to start a company after graduation. Two years later one of her professors connected her with a new client who wound up purchasing about $2 million in services from her company.

- Although Ashley was happily employed, she'd always dreamed of working at Google. A member of our career-services team was at a conference and sat next to a Google recruiter. That evening she connected them via email, and a few months later Ashley found herself reporting to the Googleplex for the first day of her new career.

- Dan was recently promoted to a leadership position and needed to hire three managers immediately. Instead of going through recruiters and recruiting websites, he reached out to our career-services team and that afternoon had the resumes of our top students and recent graduates. He wound up hiring four graduates and two interns from the program. His hires did very well, and he was commended for building a high-quality team in record time.

An active and well-connected network is one of the main benefits of an MBA program. Your MBA network should be your first stop when looking for career opportunities, new customers, new employees, or logistical support in foreign countries. However with those privileges also comes responsibility.

Your MBA network should be your first stop when looking for career opportunities, new customers, new employees, or logistical support in foreign countries.

Alumni are the greatest ambassadors a program has. Although it's fine to utilize the network when needed, it's also important to nurture it as well. Here are some great ways to do so:

- If your program hasn't already done so, create a LinkedIn page for your graduating class. This is an easy way to help interested classmates stay connected. Encourage them to post job opportunities, industry insights, or other topics of interest to the group.

- If your company has a formal relationship with your school, ask to join the recruiting team. This will allow you to interact with current students and share your experiences with them. If your company doesn't yet have a recruiting partnership with your school, explore informal mechanisms to recruit graduates and interns.

- Talk to faculty about speaking in class. Often, professors like to have recent alumni speak about relevant issues being faced by professionals in the industry about which they teach.

- Offer to mentor current students interested in working in your industry.

- Offer to speak with prospective students about the benefits of the program they are considering. Prospective students are often most interested in which program will provide them with the best postgraduation job opportunities. Meeting with successful alumni makes it easier for them to visualize their success in your program and beyond.

- Fill out all surveys sent to you from the ranking agencies. Your responses help determine your program's ranking. Alumni ask me all the time how they can help the program. Few realize one of the best ways they can improve the ranking of our program is to complete these surveys when requested.

- Join the alumni association. This is a great way to stay connected with the entire university community beyond your MBA program.

- If your company is hiring either full-time employees or interns, communicate this information to the career-services team. In addition, let them know about any changes in your career. Promotions, especially for young alumni at highly desirable organizations, make great stories to discuss with prospective students.

- Consider giving back financially to your program, even if it's just a small amount. Alumni donations help support world-class faculty, facilities, and experiences for students and also help boost the reputation of the program. Some rankings take the alumni giving rate into consideration. Many companies will match employee donations to higher education institutions.

These activities not only make a huge difference for current students but also help promote the quality of the brand. Successful alumni stories can be utilized in marketing pieces and campaigns to prospective students. Alumni who are willing to speak with prospective students can make all the difference during the recruitment process. Letters of recommendation from engaged alumni go a long way toward helping applicants in the admissions process. Current students often tell me that mentorship and job-shadow opportunities from alumni are among the most helpful resources they have.

Key Takeaways

Your relationship with your MBA program shouldn't end at graduation. Staying connected has many benefits for both you and the program. Time spent working with prospective and current students is an investment that can result in a better brand. Alumni who recruit prospective students, connect students with job opportunities, and complete surveys from the ranking agencies can help improve the ranking of their program. In addition, keeping in touch with classmates, faculty, and program staff can be advantageous to you when changing jobs, hiring new employees, or starting a new business.

Activity

After you graduate with a great job, come back to campus and meet with at least five first-year students. See if they have any questions and if the students are interested, offer to share your experiences. Determine whether anyone in your professional network can help with their professional goals and, if so, facilitate introductions as appropriate. Stay in touch with these students throughout their time in the program.

Reflection Questions

1. How do I plan to stay connected with my program after graduation?

2. Does my company have a formal recruiting relationship with my MBA program?

3. Do I know how to contact most, if not all, of my classmates?

4. What faculty and program staff do I plan to stay in touch with?

Now What?

We're done! Hopefully, you had a wonderful experience in your MBA program, landed a great job, and are actively contributing to the community of learning on campus.

SOME FINAL THOUGHTS

With the exceptions of some changed names and identifying details, the stories I've shared throughout this book are true. I hope they illustrate for you some of the critical decisions and actions that often make the difference between a successful and unsuccessful MBA experience. I hope you find the lessons to be great learning tools.

Moreover, I hope I'm leaving you with more than just a checklist of what not to do. I hope you're also left with a greater sense of confidence and control over your own MBA destiny and with optimism about the transformational potential of the degree. In particular, I hope you're convinced that there are some simple strategies that everyone—from prospective students to alumni—can use to maximize the MBA experience.

I wish I'd had a guide like this one as an MBA student. I certainly made some mistakes of my own (I could write another book about those). Still, getting an MBA has undoubtedly been the best career decision I've ever made.

Wherever you are in your MBA journey, I wish you the best of luck in your academic and professional pursuits.

Sincerely,
Brian Precious
brian@brianprecious.com

ACKNOWLEDGMENTS

It takes a village to raise a child—and apparently to write a book. I was able to take this idea from concept to reality only because of the overwhelming encouragement and support of friends, colleagues, students, family members, and professional mentors. In no particular order, I would like to thank Sean Precious, Tad Brinkerhoff, Wade George, Stephan Seyfert, Greg Olson, Tony Sarnecki, Mark Lockwood, Dr. J. Kendall Middaugh II, Tom Precious, Dr. Keith Leavitt, Ben Johnson, Jenn Casey, Mark Herdering, Ryan Lefever, Victoria Maldonado, Benny Kuo, Dr. Scott Paja, John Byrne, and Mark Shelton for their immeasurable contributions to this effort.

I also deeply appreciate my parents, Dan and Sheila Precious, for their support of the book and, more generally, in all of my professional and personal endeavors.

The many students, too, who have shared their stories,

dreams, goals, successes, and setbacks with me over the last six years deserve my sincerest gratitude. You were my inspiration.

Last, and certainly not least, my wife, Cheryl Precious, deserves much of the credit for what you have just read. She believed in me and my ability to write this book long before I did, and for that, I will be forever grateful.

APPENDIX

GMAT SCORE ANALYSIS

Comparison of Top Ten Enrollment vs.
GMAT Test Takers Scoring above 700

UNIVERSITY NAME	SCHOOL NAME	U.S. NEWS 2016 RANKING	AVG GMAT	TOTAL ENROLLMENT	DERIVATION
Stanford University		1	732	825	
Harvard University		2	726	1,867	
University of Pennsylvania	Wharton	3	728	1,711	
University of Chicago	Booth	4	724	1,181	
Massachusetts Institute of Technology	Sloan	5	713	812	
Northwestern University	Kellogg	6	713	1,047	
University of California, Berkeley	Haas	7	717	503	
Columbia University		8	716	1,270	
Dartmouth College	Tuck	9	716	558	
University of Virginia	Darden	10	706	633	
Total Seats				10,407	
Seats Available Each Year				5,204	Half of total enrollment (2-year MBA program)

Source: *U.S. News & World Report*, Best Graduate Schools 2016

Total GMATs taken in 2014   **243,529**
Source: GMAC (online benchmarking tool)

Percentage of exams by unique test takers   **80%**
Source: GMAC (2013 Profile of GMAT Candidates report)

Estimated number of unique test takers   **194,823**
Derivation: 80% of total exams administered

GMAT TOTAL SCORE PERCENTILES

PERCENTILE	SCORE	NUMBER OF STUDENTS	DERIVATION
99%	760 and above	1,948	1% of unique test takers
98%	750	3,896	2% of unique test takers
97%	740	5,845	3% of unique test takers
96%	730	7,793	4% of unique test takers
95%			
94%	720	11,689	6% of unique test takers
93%			
92%	710	15,586	8% of unique test takers
91%			
90%			
89%	700	21,431	11% of unique test takers

Source: GMAC (online benchmarking tool)

ABOUT THE AUTHOR

Brian Precious has managed the admissions, recruiting, and marketing teams at three major MBA programs—Oregon State University, Purdue University, and, his alma mater, the University of Illinois. Throughout his career in higher education, he's helped thousands of prospective MBA students navigate the challenges of business school. From casual chats at MBA fairs to formal admissions interviews and Skype conversations with students across the globe, Brian is committed to seeing his students succeed—both in business school and in their chosen careers.

Prior to his career in higher education, Brian worked as a management consultant and as the Director of Marketing for a solar electronics start-up.

Brian's passion for business school education stems from his own experiences as a student in the Illinois MBA program from

2004-2006. During that time, he gained the skills required to change careers, had the opportunity to start a company, travel the world, and make some of the most enduring friendships of his life.

Brian currently lives in Corvallis, Oregon with his wife, Cheryl; their son, Sam; and their furry son, Miles. *Get In, Get Connected, Get Hired* is his first book.